The Effective Teacher's Guide

TEACHING PRACTICES THAT WORK

Diane Lapp and Douglas Fisher, Series Editors

Designed specifically for busy teachers who value evidence-based instructional practices, books in this series offer ready-to-implement strategies and tools to promote student engagement, improve teaching and learning across the curriculum, and support the academic growth of all students in our increasingly diverse schools. Written by expert authors with extensive experience in "real-time" classrooms, each concise and accessible volume provides useful explanations and examples to guide instruction, as well as step-by-step methods and reproducible materials, all in a convenient large-size format for ease of photocopying.

35 Strategies for Guiding Readers through Informational Texts
Barbara Moss and Virginia S. Loh

**The Effective Teacher's Guide, Second Edition:
50 Ways to Engage Students and Promote Interactive Learning**
Nancy Frey

**Dare to Differentiate, Third Edition:
Vocabulary Strategies for All Students**
Danny Brassell

The Effective Teacher's Guide

50 Ways to Engage Students and Promote Interactive Learning

Second Edition

Nancy Frey

Series Editors' Note
by Diane Lapp and Douglas Fisher

THE GUILFORD PRESS
New York   London

© 2011 The Guilford Press
A Division of Guilford Publications, Inc.
72 Spring Street, New York, NY 10012
www.guilford.com

Printed in the United States of America

This book is printed on acid-free paper.

Last digit is print number: 9   8   7   6   5   4   3   2   1

Library of Congress Cataloging-in-Publication Data

Frey, Nancy, 1959–
    The effective teacher's guide : 50 ways to engage students and promote
interactive learning / Nancy Frey. — 2nd ed.
        p.   cm. — (Teaching practices that work)
    Includes bibliographical references and index.
    ISBN 978-1-60623-971-1 (pbk. : alk. paper)
    1. Effective teaching.   2. Teacher–student relationships.   3. Motivation in
education.   I. Title.
    LB1025.3.F75 2011
    371.102—dc22
                                                                        2010033171

••

About the Author

Nancy Frey, PhD, is Professor of Literacy in the School of Teacher Education at San Diego State University. She is the recipient of the 2008 Early Career Achievement Award from the National Reading Conference, as well as a co-recipient of the Christa McAuliffe Award for Excellence in Teacher Education from the American Association of State Colleges and Universities. In addition to publishing with her colleague Douglas Fisher, Dr. Frey teaches a variety of courses in San Diego State's teacher-credentialing and reading specialist programs on elementary and secondary reading instruction, literacy in content areas, and supporting students with diverse learning needs. She is a credentialed special educator and reading specialist in California and is privileged to learn with and from students and teachers at Health Sciences High and Middle College every day.

Series Editors' Note

As our schools continue to grow in linguistic, cultural, and socioeconomic diversity, educators are committed to implementing instruction that supports both individual and collective growth within their classrooms. In tandem with teacher commitment, schools recognize the need to support teacher collaboration on issues related to implementing, evaluating, and expanding instruction to ensure that all students will graduate from high school with the skills needed to succeed in the workforce. Through our work with teachers across the country, we've become aware of the need for books that can be used to support professional collaboration by grade level and subject area. With these teachers' questions in mind, we decided that a series of books was needed that modeled "real-time" teaching and learning within classroom instruction. Thus the series *Teaching Practices That Work* was born.

Books in this series are distinguished by offering instructional examples that have been studied and refined within authentic classroom settings. Each book is written by one or more educators who are well connected to everyday classroom instruction. Because the series editors are themselves classroom teachers as well as professors, each instructional suggestion has been closely scrutinized for its validity.

If you've ever wondered how to design, implement, and manage instruction that keeps students engaged in learning, you'll find a plethora of useful ideas for K–12 classrooms in this second edition of *The Effective Teacher's Guide: 50 Ways to Engage Students and Promote Interactive Learning,* by Nancy Frey. Whether you're a new teacher or one with many years of experience, this text presents easy-to-implement best practices that will help you establish and monitor a classroom management plan that supports small-group and whole-class learning. Dr. Frey uses a gradual release-of-responsibility model of instructional design to illustrate how to introduce a concept and then support students as they move toward independence as learners. Classroom-tested examples are included that have a strong research base and provide answers to your management questions. The "how-to" of integrating and managing new literacies, such as building a course website, is also explained in this edition.

We invite you into the "real-time" teaching offered in this book and hope you'll find this series useful as you validate and expand your teaching repertoire. And if you have an idea for a book, please contact us!

DIANE LAPP
DOUGLAS FISHER

Introduction
Why Is Engagement Critical to Learning?

Ms. Alvarez has the fourth graders spellbound. They lean forward in their seats, eyes fixed on their teacher as she reads expressively from *James and the Giant Peach* (Dahl, 2001). They have been listening to this enchanting story read aloud to them each day for the last 2 weeks. During that time they have explored ideas in pairs, written important passages in reading journals, and learned to use several graphic organizers to sort out their comprehension of this fantasy text. Today Ms. Alvarez will finish the novel, an event eagerly anticipated by these 9- and 10-year-olds. "And James Henry Trotter, who once, if you remember, had been the saddest and loneliest little boy you could find, now had all the friends and playmates in the world. And because so many of them were always begging him to tell and tell again the story of his adventures on the peach, he thought it would be nice if one day he sat down and wrote a book. And so he did. And that is what you have just finished reading" (Dahl, 2001, pp. 145–146). She reads the last lines reverently and then shares a sigh with her listeners. "Boys and girls, think about the best word to describe how you're feeling right at this moment." Students around the room close their eyes to ponder this question more deeply. "Now tell your partner to your left what that word is." Miriam's eyes sparkle as she leans in to whisper to Joe, her partner. "Satisfied!"

Indeed, satisfying learning experiences are what all teachers strive for in their instruction each day. Satisfying learning experiences require that students pay attention. Attention, engagement, and interaction are all crucial to keep students motivated and not left behind. Thankfully, there are specific behaviors teachers can use to ensure that learning experiences are satisfying, and result in increased understanding and achievement. Let's take a look at learning and how this is accomplished.

Learning: Memory, Attention, Engagement, and Interaction

Learning is a complex cognitive behavior that has been the subject of thousands of studies. Learning involves memory systems and attention, both of which occur in the brain. The human memory system is divided into several components, the first of which is sensory memory. Sensory memory is the ability to retain input from sensory systems after the stimulus is gone. Sensory memory is brief, in terms of time, but critical for learning. Just think about students who haven't learned to process the input they receive from their eyes or ears; they have a hard time learning!

In addition to sensory memory, learning requires the use of working memory. Formerly called "short-term" memory, this system is defined as

> a system for temporarily storing and managing the information required to carry out complex cognitive tasks such as learning, reasoning, and comprehension. Working memory is involved in the selection, initiation, and termination of information-processing functions such as encoding, storing, and retrieving data. (*www.medterms.com*)

It's pretty easy to see how working memory influences learning. It's the manipulation of information and the connection of new information with information already stored in the brain that causes learning. In essence, we use our working memory to hold bits of information that we might or might not need to transfer to long-term memory. Of course, as teachers, we want all of our content to transfer to students' long-term memory. Unfortunately, the brain is pretty good at filtering information and it's harder to get information across the barrier than most people believe.

Long-term memory, what most people think of as remembering, is even more complex. Not much is known, really, about long-term memory other than the fact that pathways are formed and that accessing these pathways again triggers remembering. Some of the best ways to ensure storage in long-term memory involves rehearsal and meaningful associations. And much of the classroom practices today involve students rehearsing (practicing) and associating (applying). Long-term memory has been further subdivided into two categories: declarative, which can be subdivided into episodic and semantic, and procedural. All of these are relevant for teachers as we work across types of memory to get to learning. (For more information about memory, see *Brain Rules* by John Medina, 2008.)

Now let's consider attention. In terms of learning, attention requires that the person concentrate on a specific feature of the environment and essentially ignore the others. If you are paying attention to what you read in this book, your brain has filtered out the feel of your clothes, the hum of the light above your head, and the taste of the gum you're chewing. Medina (2008) reminds us that it is biologically impossible to learn and remember information that the brain has not paid any attention to. It's also important to recognize that the brain isn't designed to pay attention to the same thing for extended periods of time but rather to notice novel stimuli. And to quote Medina, "We don't pay attention to boring things" (p. 71).

Teachers know that attention and memory are related and thus focus efforts on student engagement. And I think that engagement—paying attention—is important. However, the emphasis on engagement—paying attention—somehow was confounded with compliance. Administrators sometimes rated teachers based on the percentage of students "engaged" in the lesson, but in truth this was measured only by outward behaviors like sitting quietly and facing forward. In turn, the "good" classrooms were understood to be the quiet ones. This held repercussions for individual students as well. Being a "good" student meant that you were quiet and well behaved. What happened inside the brain was less valued than compliance.

But something happened along the way. The world changed, and with it came a different mindset about teaching and learning. You would be hard-pressed to find an administrator today who thinks that a quiet classroom is a good one. Instead, he or she would be troubled by the lack of oral language. It would be difficult to locate a teacher today who didn't think that Vygotsky (1978) got it right when he wrote about zones of proximal development (and the implications related to scaffolded instruction). And yet, too many classrooms are still dominated by instructional practices that favor compliance over interaction. The difference is that now students arrive at our classroom doors with a belief that they can direct their own learning. For many, school has become something to be endured. We inadvertently reinforce this notion every time we tell them "you'll need this in the real world." When did school stop being a part of the real world?

It stops every time classroom learning becomes too removed from the learning that occurs throughout the rest of the day. Ask someone where to find information on Genghis Khan, and he or she will likely search the Internet (and often on a personal digital assistant, or PDA). Ask someone when his or her next meeting is, and he or she will use the electronic calendar on his or her mobile phone. Ask someone about a protest somewhere in the world, and he or she will check out Twitter. And yet in too many classrooms, these tools are forbidden. "Too distracting," we're told, which is just another way of saying that we believe learning is a silent and solitary activity. We need to move beyond *engagement*, which is a start but doesn't go far enough for learning. We need to focus on *interaction* as the real gold standard for learning.

From Engagement to Interaction

Consider the contrast between those two words: *engagement* and *interaction*. A comparison of dictionary definitions is instructive. Engagement refers to the ability to attract attention and then hold on to it. But then what? We've all witnessed engagement. It can be that slack-jawed look that comes over the face of an adolescent watching a film in class. He's engaged all right, but it's passive. He is a consumer of information, but nothing more. "Interaction kicks it up a notch," as chef Emeril Lagasse would say. The dictionary defines interaction as having an effect on one another. It's reciprocal, and it acknowledges the necessary presence of another entity.

Consult a thesaurus to evaluate the difference in synonyms for the two terms. Synonyms for engagement include words like *captivate, charm*, and *enthrall*. Compare these terms to the synonyms for interaction: *communicate, collaborate*, and *connect*. Engagement is one-way, while interaction is two-way. Table 1 shows a comparison of the two words.

My purpose is not to broker an esoteric discussion on semantics. Rather, it is to foreground interaction as an important component of learning. Interaction is at the heart of the biggest advance so far of this young century—Web 2.0. Beginning in the first part of the decade, the World Wide Web moved "from publishing to participation" (Flew, 2008). First-generation websites were seen as a vehicle for disseminating information, and in this way performed similarly to print libraries. The notion that "everything you need to know is on the Internet" was born out of this (somewhat misguided) impression. But the advent of second-generation technologies shifted the focus to the user—you may even recall that "You" were the Person of the Year for *Time* magazine in 2006. The ability to act upon information, not just passively consume it, has become the bright line that changes everything. Is it any wonder that students arrive at the schoolhouse expecting to act upon information?

TABLE 1. Comparing *Engagement* and *Interaction*

	Engage	*Interact*
Dictionary definition	to attract, hold fast, occupy attention of another or oneself	to act one upon another, to have some effect on each other
Prefix	*en*: to cause a person to be in . . . (a state, condition, place)	among, between, mutually, reciprocally
Root	*gage*: (archaic) a pledge, a challenge, deposit	*act*: to do something, exert energy or force, produce an effect
Spanish translation	*ocupar*	*relacionarse* (interaction: *acción recíproca*)
Synonyms	captivate, charm, employ, enthrall, involve, join, practice	collaborate, combine, communicate, connect, cooperate

Why This Book?

Engagement and interaction involve the ability to gain and maintain students' attention in order for them to increase knowledge and understanding. Together, these influence two critical aspects of a teacher's day: management and learning. Of course, management and learning are inexorably intertwined with one another. Numerous studies have demonstrated that the use of routines and procedures contributes positively to learning and the smooth operation of a classroom (Emmer, Evertson, & Anderson, 1980; Evertson & Harris, 1999). The secret is to be familiar with these routines as well as with how to implement them in the classroom. Part One of this book discusses five guiding principles for engaging students throughout each and every lesson you teach. These principles address organization, active participation, interaction, and the ways in which students help and learn from one another. These guiding principles serve as a foundation for the subsequent sections.

Part Two looks at the practical considerations for creating and establishing a classroom management plan. The strategies in Part Three address the organization of students and materials, while Part Four addresses the role of peer partners in learning. Part Five is filled with methods for engaging students in learning. Finally, Part Six closes the book with a close look at engagement through reading. Taken together, these 50 practices can ensure a good start to the school year for a beginning teacher or transform the teaching day for an experienced teacher who may have forgotten some of these time-proven strategies.

References

Dahl, R. (2001). *James and the giant peach.* New York: Puffin.

Emmer, E., Evertson, C., & Anderson, L. (1980). Effective classroom management at the beginning of the school year. *Elementary School Journal, 80,* 219–231.

Evertson, C., & Harris, A. (1999). Support for managing learning-centered classrooms: The classroom organization and management program. In H. J. Frieberg (Ed.), *Beyond behaviorism: Changing the classroom management paradigm* (pp. 59–74). Boston: Allyn & Bacon.

Flew, T. (2008). *New media: An introduction* (3rd ed.). Melbourne, Australia: Oxford University Press. Retrieved from *en.wikipedia.org/wiki/Web_1.0.*

MedicineNet.com. (n.d.). Definition of short-term memory. Retrieved from *www. medterms.com/scripts/main/art.asp?articlekey=7142.*

Medina, J. (2008). *Brain rules: 12 principles for surviving and thriving at work, home, and school.* Seattle, WA: Pear Press.

Time. (2006, December 13). Time's person of the year: You. Retrieved from *www. time.com/time/magazine/article/0,9171,1569514,00.html.*

Vygotsky, L. S. (1978). *Mind in society* (M. Cole, V. John-Steiner, S. Scribner, & E. Souberman, Eds.). Cambridge, MA: Harvard University Press.

Contents

PART ONE

Five Rules for Engagement and Interaction

PART TWO

Engaging Students through Classroom Procedures

PART THREE

Engaging Students through Organization

PART FOUR

Engaging Students through Peer Partners

PART FIVE

Engaging Students for Learning

PART SIX

Engaging Students through Reading

PART ONE

Five Rules
for Engagement
and Interaction

1

Organize Your Instruction through Gradual Release of Responsibility

GRADE LEVELS: K–12

What Is It?

Organizing instruction using a gradual release of responsibility model allows teachers to intentionally plan to move from providing extensive support to allowing students to be supported by peers before completing tasks independently with no teacher support (Pearson & Gallagher, 1983). Or as Duke and Pearson (2002) suggest, teachers have to move from assuming "all the responsibility for performing a task . . . to a situation in which the students assume all of the responsibility" (p. 211). This principle guides effective instruction regardless of grade level or content because it echoes what Good and Brophy (2003) call "active teaching." Active teaching is the ability of an educator to present information to learners in ways that are effective and do not waste the students' time. When learners are in the presence of someone who has mastered active teaching, they (Fisher & Frey, 2008):

- Understand the purpose of the lesson.
- See the skill or strategy modeled.
- Practice it under the guidance of the teacher.
- Consolidate understanding with peers.
- Practice independently.

The format can be easily captured in these memorable statements:

I do it. (Modeling)
We do it. (Guided Instruction)
You do it together. (Collaborative Learning)
You do it alone. (Independent Tasks)

What Do I Do?

Modeling: I Do It

In the first phase of the lesson, the teacher explains the purpose of the lesson and models the instructional task while students watch closely. Whether the skill being taught is to locate the main idea in a paragraph, throw a wedged ball of clay onto a potter's wheel, or complete a quadratic formula, the first step of good instruction is an expert showing the apprentices how it's done (see Figure 1.1 for a map of how these three lessons are taught using this framework). During this time teachers may use a think-aloud strategy (Davey, 1983) by vocalizing the thinking processes they are using as they complete the task, in particular how they make decisions related to

Task / Lesson Phase	Find the Main Idea	Throw a Pot	Complete a Quadratic Equation
Modeling: I do it.	Teacher locates main idea in a paragraph projected on the overhead and discusses why. A think-aloud strategy is employed so students can gain insight into a reader's decision- making process.	Teacher is seated at a potter's wheel and explains the techniques for locating the center of a spinning wheel while demonstrating. A think-aloud strategy is employed so students can gain insight into a potter's decision-making process.	Teacher demonstrates technique for moving the constant in an equation and completing the square to solve. A think-aloud strategy is employed so students can gain insight into a mathematician's problem-solving process.
Guided Instruction: We do it together.	Teacher meets with small groups to coach them through a problem and uses prompts and cues to resolve confusing parts.	Teacher meets with small groups to coach them through a problem and uses prompts and cues to resolve confusing parts.	Teacher meets with small groups to coach them through a problem and uses prompts and cues to resolve confusing parts.
Collaborative Learning: You do it together.	Students work in pairs with a common text to find the main idea together.	Students work in pairs, taking turns at a wheel while one throws the clay and the other closely observes and gives feedback.	Students work in pairs to solve another quadratic equation together.
Independent Tasks: You do it alone.	Students read a series of paragraphs and locate the main ideas independently. Teacher circulates, assists, and monitors.	Students work at their own wheel to successfully throw the clay on the pot and center it. Teacher circulates, assists, and monitors.	Students work their own quadratic equation problem. Teacher circulates, assists, and monitors.

FIGURE 1.1. Gradual release of responsibility framework.

their understanding of the task. This modeling procedure may be repeated several times as the teacher gauges the level of questions generated by the students. When a sufficient level of understanding has been reached by the group, the lesson moves to the next phase.

Guided Instruction: We Do It

Once students have had the opportunity to watch a teacher complete the operation several times and ask clarifying questions about it, they are now ready to assume shared responsibility for the task with the teacher. This is a critical phase of the lesson and skipping it is bound to result in errors, frustration, and classroom management problems. This is the guided instruction all learners require as they add a new skill or strategy to their repertoire—a chance to practice the task while a more knowledgeable adult is close by to shape their attempts and prevent predictable mistakes. Typically a teacher in the "we do it" phase of the lesson will pose a short example of the task to pairs or small groups of students and then coach them as they work on it. This allows the learners to use one another as well as the teacher as a source for information. Along the way, the teacher provides prompts and cues to transfer responsibility to the students. For example, when given a sample quadratic problem, the teacher observes as students begin working. As they get stuck, the teacher prompts (e.g., "Did you remember problem number 4 and what you did there?") and cues (e.g., "Look again at the figure on page 145") such that the student is able to experience success based on the coaching provided by the teacher.

Collaborative Learning: You Do It Together

In this phase, the teacher steps aside and provides students, working in groups, with a task that allows them to consolidate their understanding. The key to collaborative learning is accountability. Each student in the group is accountable, individually, based on what the group is working on together. In addition, collaborative learning is a time in which students talk with one another using academic language. They need to practice the thinking and language presented in the lesson if they are to become proficient users of that language. For example, if the task is to throw clay on a potter's wheel to create a vase, pairs of students may take turns working at the same wheel, alternating in the role of potter and observer. They provide each other with feedback on what seems to be working and what does not. At the end of the lesson, each student has produced a vase, with the support of a peer. As a by-product, they've talked a lot about the production of the vase and have incorporated the academic language of the content area into their thinking.

Independent Tasks: You Do It Alone

At this point in the lesson, students have had a chance to watch a proficient practitioner demonstrate the task while sharing his or her decision-making processes to successfully complete the task. Next, students try on the task themselves while a peer offers support and feedback. As part of the guided instruction, the teacher provides additional technical feedback when necessary. Now the learners are ready to independently practice the task. While this independent practice often serves as the basis for homework, effective teachers tell us that the task is more likely to be completed if it is partially completed at school. While students are independently practicing the task, the teacher is once again an active participant, circulating and assisting students while monitoring progress. Remember, teaching is a stand-up, walk-around job and your role is to move about the room.

When students are guided through a thoughtful learning process that progressively allows them to take on increasing levels of work, they move smoothly from observer to active participant in the learning process. In addition, the teacher remains actively affiliated with the entire learning cycle, not just the direct instruction phase. By using this lesson frame, students with diverse abilities, skills, and experiences have the opportunity to learn and become more accomplished in academic tasks.

References

Davey, B. (1983). Think aloud: Modeling the cognitive processes for reading comprehension. *Journal of Reading, 27,* 44–47.

Duke, N., & Pearson, P. D. (2002). Effective practices for developing reading comprehension. In A. E. Farstrup & S. J. Samuels (Eds.), *What research has to say about reading instruction* (3rd ed., pp. 205–242). Newark, DE: International Reading Association.

Fisher, D., & Frey, N. (2008). *Better learning through structured teaching: A framework for the gradual release of responsibility.* Alexandria, VA: Association for Supervision and Curriculum Development.

Good, T. L., & Brophy, J. E. (2003). *Looking in classrooms* (9th ed.). Boston: Allyn & Bacon.

Pearson, P. D., & Gallagher, G. (1983). The gradual release of responsibility model of instruction. *Contemporary Educational Psychology, 8,* 112–123.

2

Active Engagement Is Multileveled
Group–Partner–Individual

GRADE LEVELS: K–12

What Is It?

This rule is closely related to the first one, and in fact you'll see that it is imbedded in the gradual release of responsibility instructional framework. When I refer to multileveled I mean that learning opportunities are experienced in a series of student grouping arrangements. First, students observe as the teacher models and then they try the task themselves as they work in pairs to collaboratively solve the problem. Finally, students can practice the new skill or strategy individually.

The most common grouping arrangement in classrooms is whole-group instruction. There are important reasons for conducting whole-group instruction. In particular, this is an effective format for presenting new information to a class and leading discussions. In fact, that's how you should think of whole-group instruction—a means for presentation and discussion. However, without some strategies for increasing active participation by the group, involvement will be limited to the most academically and socially sure members of the class. Many other students will be left out in the process.

An additional problem is that for some teachers the grouping format rarely varies from this model. Therefore, students have no opportunity to figure things out with another learner or to hear what that partner can offer. This is where partner work comes in. In terms of instructional flow, it works especially well during the "you do it together" phase. However, partner work can also occur across the lesson, so I'll discuss those strategies as well.

I'll also share methods for active participation at the individual level. While much of the work of active participation centers on what happens in partners, it is essential that this learning translates to involvement by each student. This is critical for students who bring a variety of learning strengths and needs to your classroom, especially those who are English language learners (ELLs) or possess an individualized education plan (IEP) because of a physical or cognitive disability.

Inclusive Active Participation

A central goal for every teacher is to continually elicit responses from students. Highly effective teachers know that the responses need to be inclusive—they allow for *every* student in the class to participate. This is a fundamental precept of teaching—every student needs to belong in the flow of the classroom instruction. Response demands that do not allow for the inclusion of every student serve to marginalize the child in the eyes of their classmates because the unspoken message is "your thoughts, ideas, and opinions don't matter to us." This is a devastating message to teach and one that no one intentionally plans; however, the message is the same whether it is deliberate or not.

> Active participation by all students benefits the teacher because it allows for three important channels of information:
>
> Feedback on student learning.
> ⇩
> Ability to adjust the lesson.
> ⇩
> More systematic presentation of information to students.

There are important benefits for students as well. Students who are required to respond frequently in a lesson are more attentive. In addition, they receive more practice of the skill or strategy being taught. And as every good classroom manager knows, increased participation means increased accountability. It's more difficult to be off-task if your teacher is asking you to do something every few minutes! But of course the ultimate goal is more than just classroom management—it's learning. Here's another formula to remember:

Attention + Practice + Accountability = LEARNING

What Do I Do?

Active Participation: Group

One of the easiest ways to increase participation with a group of students is to have them respond verbally. These choral responses to questions raised by the teacher are meant to reinforce key information through oral rehearsal. The responses should be brief (one to three words) and be elicited after the answer has been taught. The teacher elicits this verbal response by signaling the class with a gesture that has been previously taught (see Chapter 17, Signaling the Class, for more information). Here's what a sequence might look and sound like:

TEACHER: The water molecule is composed of hydrogen and oxygen. [Present information]

TEACHER: Boys and girls, the water molecule is composed of what? [Ask question]

TEACHER: (*Raises hand and pauses to allow think time.*)

TEACHER: (*Drops hand.*)

STUDENTS: Hydrogen and oxygen.

The key things to remember with this kind of response are to first state the information and then pose the question. Signal the class by using a gesture that has been taught, for instance, raising a hand in the air. Remember to hold the gesture to allow for thinking time and then give the next signal (e.g., dropping the hand) to elicit the choral response. By interspersing your lecture with these response opportunities, you gain feedback on the status of the learning that's occurring. If the response is incorrect or weak, repeat the information and pose the question again. This kind of rehearsal of new information primes your students for the guided and independent practice to come. For more ideas about eliciting responses, see Chapter 42, Response Cards, later in this book.

Active Participation: Partner

The most important benefit of partnering is that it increases participation by all students because it is a safe way to share. Not every student is eager to state his or her knowledge and opinions in front of the entire class. These students may be English Language Learners who are uncomfortable with their command of the language or students with communication disabilities. And don't overlook the shy or reticent student who is reluctant to speak in front of the larger group. The fact is that there are many undercurrents in the social and psychological dynamics of a classroom that the teacher is not privy to. When a teacher uses partner work, the number of responses increases. Keep in mind that every response does not need to channel through the teacher. When a teacher asks a question and one student answers, there are 29 responses that never had a chance to occur. When the question is answered in partners, 30 responses occur. It's a matter of mathematics:

1 question × 2 partners = 30 responses

There are academic benefits as well. In addition to increasing participation by all, partners make the answer more complete because they are able to clarify and refine the understanding each has of the concept being taught. Therefore, students who have had the chance to rehearse their answers with a partner are more confident in reporting answers to the class. This is especially true of students learning English because they can practice and correct their expressive language before attempting it in front of the larger group. It goes without saying that communicating with a partner allows for practice of receptive language skills as well.

Partners can work together in a variety of ways to rehearse what they are learning. A few examples include

- Observe each other doing a physical education (PE) skill.
- Work on solving a math problem together.
- Edit each other's written work.
- Complete a science experiment together.

Like all classroom routines, partnering procedures need to be explicitly taught in order to ensure a smooth operation. It is these routines that hold a benefit for the overall management of the classroom because when provided with authorized time to speak to each other, it actually reduces unauthorized talk. It is helpful to have a method for assigning partners quickly so that lost academic time is kept to a minimum.

Active Participation: Individual

Students in effective classrooms move from teacher modeling to partner learning to clarify their understanding of skills and concepts. Eventually they work individually as they move toward proficiency. However, work at the individual level presents a new set of management challenges to the teacher. In particular, students working independently need to pace themselves properly, possess strategies for gaining assistance, and remain organized. Throughout this book you will find many ideas for teaching students these strategies. In all cases, the intent of these engagement strategies is to scaffold instruction so learners can eventually use them independently.

3

Instruction Is Interactive
Say–Write–Do

GRADE LEVELS: K–12

What Is It?

This rule refers to the elements of engagement and interaction necessary in every lesson. Good instruction demands that every teaching event involve students as active participants in their own learning, which also allows the teacher to plan subsequent lessons based on students' understandings and misunderstandings (Fisher & Frey, 2009). This does not mean that your classroom must become a dance studio where students are constantly moving from one place to another (although movement is important in learning). Instead, I mean that the instruction is interactive because in each lesson students have the opportunity to say things, write things, and do things. The use of multiple modalities of learning reinforces the skills you are teaching and increases the likelihood that they will recall the information later (Ellis, Semb, & Cole, 1998).

What Do I Do?

Students Say Things

During all phases of instruction, students need to speak in order to repeat new vocabulary, answer questions, and practice new information. For example, during group instruction the teacher can signal students to repeat a key phrase by first asking a question, signaling the class to get ready for a group response, pausing for thinking time, then signaling again to respond in unison.

TEACHER: In what year was the Declaration of Independence signed?

The teacher raises one hand palm up to signal to the class that they should get ready for a group response, then pauses for a few seconds for wait time.

TEACHER: Everyone.

The teacher now lowers the raised hand to signal the response.

CLASS: 1776.

Note that you have read about this technique already in the previous chapter. Good engagement practices accomplish multiple goals simultaneously.

Another method for fostering student responses during group instruction is to invite students to share their response with a partner. Teach students that your signal to "turn to a partner" is their cue to answer the question that has just been posed. To ensure both partners have an opportunity, make sure that partnerships are assigned within your seating chart. You can then prompt not only the question but also who will answer.

TEACHER: Partner 1, in what year was the Declaration of Independence signed? Turn to partner 2 to answer.

Students turn to face one another and all the students designated as partner 1 answer, "1776."

TEACHER: Partner 2, who was the major author of this document? Turn to partner 1 to answer.

Students again face one another and all the partner 2 students answer, "Thomas Jefferson."

Students Write Things

Another modality for reinforcing key concepts and skills involves writing during the lesson. Students can be instructed to write words or statements directly in their notebook while the teacher circulates to check for accuracy. Instruct students to put down their pen or pencil after they have written their answer so the lesson can be properly paced.

Response boards are particularly effective for monitoring what is written. Each student has a small whiteboard and washable board marker at his or her desk. Throughout the lesson, the teacher instructs students to write answers to questions and hold up their response board. This provides an opportunity to assess the knowledge of the class and clear up misunderstandings.

Students Do Things

In addition to speaking and writing during lessons, students do things. This is evidenced primarily through having them touch an item with their finger or pencil to indicate their response. An advantage of this type of engagement is that it allows the teacher to monitor rates of participation and attention. Students can be instructed to locate a city on a map, find the directions on a worksheet, or point to the topic sentence in a reading passage.

Learners can also use a series of hand signals to indicate their response. The most basic is the "thumbs up, thumbs down" signal for dichotomous choices. More complex questions can be answered using "Fist to Five." Students use the correct number of fingers to indicate their level of agreement or disagreement with a particular statement.

Fist to Five

- **Fist.** "This topic is new to me and I need more information before I make a choice."
- **One finger.** "I completely disagree with this statement and can offer several reasons to support my position."
- **Two fingers.** "I disagree with this statement and can offer one reason to support my position."
- **Three fingers.** "I am unsure of where I stand on this issue and am interested in hearing from others."
- **Four fingers.** "I agree with this statement and can offer one reason to support my position."
- **Five fingers.** "I completely agree with this statement and can offer several reasons to support my position."

References

Ellis, J., Semb, G., & Cole, B. (1998). Very long-term memory for information taught in school. *Contemporary Educational Psychology, 23,* 419–433.

Fisher, D., & Frey, N. (2009). Feed up, back, forward. *Educational Leadership, 67*(3), 20–25.

4

Students Help Each Other
Tell–Help–Check

GRADE LEVELS: K–12

What Is It?

Evidence on the effectiveness of student collaboration for learning has been well documented in research literature (Johnson, Johnson, & Maruyama, 1983; Slavin, 1996). When students work together in productive ways, learning improves (Frey, Fisher, & Everlove, 2009). However, some students may be unsure of how to work together to support each other's learning. They can benefit from a structure for reviewing material to reinforce their learning. This structure, called tell–help–check, provides such a frame to use during instruction.

What Do I Do?

Periodically during the lesson, ask students to restate or review important concepts to one another using this pattern. For example, during a science lecture on states of matter, the teacher asks students to name and summarize the four states discussed.

- **Tell.** Partner 1 turns to partner 2 and recalls the information without using notes or textbooks.
- **Help.** Partner 2 listens carefully and asks questions and gives hints about any missing or incorrect information.
- **Check.** Both partners consult notes, textbook, or handouts to confirm accuracy of information.

In addition to serving as a collaborative task, tell–help–check builds the community in the classrooms. This is important as students learn that they can rely on others for help and guidance and that they don't have to hide the fact that they might not yet understand the content. A positive classroom climate, especially one that is filled with interaction and peer support, contributes to student achievement and success later in life.

References

Frey, N., Fisher, D., & Everlove, S. (2009). *Productive group work: How to engage students, build teamwork, and promote understanding.* Alexandria, VA: Association for Supervision and Curriculum Development.

Johnson, D., Johnson, R., & Maruyama, G. (1983). Interdependence and interpersonal attraction among heterogeneous and homogeneous individuals: A theoretical formulation and meta-analysis of the research. *Review of Educational Research, 53,* 5–54.

Slavin, R. (1996). Research on cooperative learning and achievement: What we know, what we need to know. *Contemporary Educational Psychology, 21,* 43–69.

5

Students Learn from Each Other
Think–Pair–Share

GRADE LEVELS: K–12

What Is It?

Think–pair–share is an instructional technique developed to encourage increased interaction and participation during classroom discussions (Lyman, 1981). In addition, it is intended to foster higher-quality responses by allowing students to try out their answers on a partner before sharing them with the whole class. This lowers the risk for learners while raising accountability and engagement because every student is actively involved.

What Do I Do?

There are four steps to the think–pair–share process.

1 **Pose a question to the class.** Invite discussion by first asking a thought-provoking question that requires an extended response.

2 **Think.** Prompt students to think quietly about their answer. This is similar to the brainstorming phase of a group discussion.

3 **Pair.** After the wait time, students turn to their partners to offer their response and to listen to the ideas of their peer. Once both have shared, they should ask questions and discuss the topic.

4 **Share.** Signal students to finish their discussion and focus their attention on you. Ask them to share their responses and those of their partner. This exchange of ideas should serve as the next step in your classwide discussion of the topic.

As noted in the discussion below, students often clarify their understanding during partner conversations. In addition, they often shift pronouns from "I" to "we" or "he" or "she," which is safer and involves less risk in presenting ideas to the whole class.

TEACHER: I'm thinking about race and the role it has played in history. Is race important? Turn to your partners and discuss this.

BRANDI: Yeah, race is because it's who you are. It's everything.

DESTANI: True, but we all have a race and that's something we have in common.

BRANDI: The human race? Is that what you mean?

DESTANI: Maybe we're letting race have too much power. I'm proud of my race, but maybe we need to focus on being part of the human race.

BRANDI: Maybe. But I don't get respect from some other races. They throw it in my face. It does matter.

DESTANI: That happens to me too, and it makes me mad. But what do I do but get mad? Maybe if everyone thought more about the human race, it would be better.

BRANDI: Yeah, if everyone did. It reminds me of a sticker on a car that said, "If you see yourself in others, it's hard to hurt anyone." Is that what you're saying?

TEACHER: Welcome back. I hope your conversations were productive. Anyone want to share?

BRANDI: Yeah, we thought that race really does matter, but the human race is the one more of us need to think about.

Reference

Lyman, F. T. (1981). The responsive classroom discussion: The inclusion of all students. In A. Anderson (Ed.), *Mainstreaming digest* (pp. 109–113). College Park: University of Maryland.

PART TWO

Engaging Students through Classroom Procedures

6

Creating a Classroom Management Plan

GRADE LEVELS: K–12

Time Needed: Several hours

What Is It?

A classroom management plan is a teacher-created document that captures the rules, procedures, and schedules that will be used to govern the classroom. Many principals require that all teachers submit a classroom management plan each year so that administrators and families understand how each classroom is to be managed. Committing a thoughtful and well-constructed plan to paper is a first step in a proactive approach to classroom management and can prevent problems from emerging (Kounin, 1970). It can also be a tool for you to decide in advance of a situation how you will respond. Being proactive, not reactive, is the key to good classroom management. Conroy, Sutherland, Snyder, and Marsh (2008) note that classrooms without a classwide approach to management have more instances of negative student–teacher interactions, and less time spent on academic instruction.

It is useful to understand the difference between classroom management and discipline, or behavior management. A classroom management plan outlines the procedures, routines, and expectations for all of the students in the class. These include simple routines such as retrieving and replacing materials, as well as more conceptual ideas such as the expectations about the way students interact with others and their learning environment. Discipline, or behavior management, is a component of the overall classroom management plan and is devoted to how problem behavior is prevented, as well as the approach one will use in addressing problem behavior.

Once the classroom management plan has been constructed, you can produce a child-friendly version for students and a letter home for families. This is recommended for two reasons: it serves as an initial means for welcoming students and families at the beginning of the year, and it can become a tool for discussion when a difficulty arises with a specific student. This chapter addresses many of the aspects of a sound classroom management plan. Keep your classroom management plan in mind as you read this book and note the items you want to be sure to include in it.

What Do I Do?

A good classroom management plan reflects the aspects valued by the teacher and therefore should be unique to the individual. "Canned" plans (those that have been written by someone else and made available to the public) are unlikely to meet the needs of your unique situation. However, it is useful to view a variety of these before you write your first plan so you can determine what you want to include. Ask your colleagues to share their plans so you can gain a sense of what is expected at your school. In addition, there are many resources available on the Internet. For instance, many professional organizations offer social-networking tools for teachers to discuss classroom management considerations specific to a content area. As an example, the National Council of Teachers of English (NCTE) maintains a Ning (a social network) for its members to discuss a variety of instructional issues related to the field.

Now You Try It

A basic classroom management plan should include the following elements:

◆ **A statement of your teaching and learning philosophy.** What are your views and beliefs about how teaching and learning should occur in your classroom? What are your beliefs concerning community and diversity in the classroom? Your statement should be no more than a few sentences long, yet be clear enough for administrators, students, and families to understand your teaching philosophy. Keep your audiences in mind—if you are teaching very young children, you may want to offer an appropriate version for your students. In addition, families that speak a language other than English appreciate the effort to communicate in the home language. If you are not fluent in the home language, seek assistance from your school's parent resource coordinator, parent center, or district language office for translation. This is an investment that is well worth the time.

◆ **Classroom rules.** Your rules should serve as a clear message about the expectations of behavior in your classroom. Authorities recommend limiting the number to no more than three to five positively stated rules. More details about composing rules follow.

◆ **Classroom procedures.** Every environment needs a set of procedures in order to ensure a smooth-running setting. When creating your classroom management plan, consider how students will perform basic procedures such as turning in homework, sharpening pencils, asking for help, and entering and leaving the room. A number of procedures are addressed in this part and throughout this book.

◆ **A daily and weekly schedule.** Your classroom schedule will be influenced by the organization of your school, grade level, or department. However, it is essential to create a map of the daily and weekly events that will occur, including start and dismissal times and lunch and recess scheduling. Elementary classes may attend weekly art, music, and physical education classes. Once these basic time boundaries are established, you can plan your curricular schedule. In multiple-subject classrooms, this will include reading and language arts, mathematics, social studies, and science. Be sure to consult your district and school documents to ensure you are adequately addressing these subject areas. These schedules are especially helpful for families. Consider making the daily schedule available on your classroom website or the school's. A more detailed discussion on designing and establishing a schedule can be found in Chapter 16, Posting a Daily Schedule.

◆ **Room arrangement.** Once you have outlined your curricular schedule, you can plan the physical layout of the room. Most teachers designate specific areas of the room for academic, social, and storage purposes. In addition, you will want to ensure that traffic patterns are logical and that you can easily see each student in the room (Wong & Wong, 2009). More information about arranging your room can be found later in this part.

◆ **Student absences.** This section of your plan should contain the school district's policy for absences as well as your methods for sharing work missed by students while they were gone. These may include an absence notebook, note taking, and homework buddies. In addition, you may have assignments posted on your website or classroom e-platform. All of these are discussed in more detail later in this part.

◆ **Discipline procedures.** How will you address disruptions in the classroom? How will disputes between students be resolved? What are the responses you anticipate using for a variety of infractions? Clearly stated discipline procedures that are stated in writing can prevent misunderstandings with students, families, and administrators. Again, be sure to consult school and district discipline plans to ensure you are in compliance with these regulations.

◆ **Communication plan.** Once your plan has been created, you will need to consider how you will share it with students and families. Secondary teachers often create a syllabus that is covered with students on the first day of class and may even require a parent signature. Elementary teachers are more likely to generate a simplified plan written in developmentally appropriate ("kid-friendly") language. In addition, they may send a letter home to families during the first week of school and review their procedures during the first Back-to-School Night. As stated previously, consider the developmental and language needs of your audiences, as you may need more than one version.

References

Conroy, M. A., Sutherland, K. S., Snyder, A. L., & Marsh, S. (2008). Classwide interventions: Effective instruction makes a difference. *Teaching Exceptional Children, 40*(6), 24–30.

Kounin, J. (1970). *Discipline and group management in classrooms.* New York: Holt, Rinehart & Winston.

Wong, H. K., & Wong, R. T. (2009). *The first days of school.* Mountain View, CA: Harry K. Wong.

•••••••••••••••••••••• **7** ••••••••••••••••••••••

Creating and Teaching
Classroom Rules

GRADE LEVELS: K–12

Time Needed: Several class sessions

What Is It?

Effective teachers regard classroom rules as an essential element for managing a smooth-running learning environment. Well-written rules communicate the teacher's expectations for the class as they relate to climate and student performance (Rosenthal, 1974; Wong & Wong, 2009). It is important to note that once rules are created, they must be explicitly taught to students. Two studies of efficient elementary and middle school classrooms found that in all cases the teachers taught the rules daily during the first week of school using discussion, modeling, and demonstrations (Emmer, Evertson, & Anderson, 1980; Evertson & Emmer, 1982). New technologies further increase the need for rules in digital environments. The advent of discussion boards and online collaborative tools has increased the need to ensure that students are taught the norms and expectations of how they work together, whether face-to-face or online (Staarman, 2009).

Rules also serve to convey high expectations, mutual respect, and an acknowledgment of the learning community. A set of rules that are strictly compliance based ("Raise your hand," "Don't speak unless called on") tell the students that you're the one with all the power, and they better listen or else. However, rules that emphasize a collaborative spirit ("Listen and respond respectfully, even when you disagree") signal students that learning is social and done in the company of others. It also lets students know that the role of the teacher is to foster learning, not primarily control and confine students. Classroom rules are sometimes mistakenly perceived as being necessary only for younger students, but the evidence is quite the contrary. A number of studies of adolescents has shown that well-written and enforced rules contribute positively to teacher–student relationships and increase participation of students in classroom discourse and discussion (e.g., Matsumura, Slater, & Crosson, 2008).

What Do I Do?

There are two decisions you will need to make as you draft rules for your classroom: Will the rules be developed with your students or written independently by you? Will you use rules that are specific in nature, or do you prefer general rules?

Student Collaboration or Teacher Generated?

The first decision you will need to make is whether you intend to create the rules yourself or collaborate with your students to formulate the rules for the year. Advantages of writing rules with students include building more "buy-in" because students have had input, as well as conveying an expectation that the class will operate as a community. This can lead to a sense of autonomy as students learn they are responsible for their behavior (Kohn, 1996). Remember that the teacher is a member of this community and can establish rules that he or she deem necessary. Teacher guidance in developing the rules for the class is needed in order to ensure that all aspects of the classroom day are addressed. Beginning teachers may prefer to create their own rules without student input. There is an advantage in doing so in the early years of your career. During the first years of professional practice educators are experimenting with what works and what doesn't. An advantage of writing rules in this manner is that you can ensure you are addressing the aspects you deem necessary.

Specific or General Rules?

The second decision you will need to make is whether to state the rules for your classroom using specific or general terms. Rules that are specific in nature state explicitly what the expected behavior should be. Further, they are observable and measurable to others. Examples of specific rules include:

- Raise your hand to speak in class.
- Enter the classroom quietly and put away your belongs.
- Keep hands and feet to yourself.
- Use a quiet voice.

A disadvantage of using specific rules is that it can lead to the "loophole defense" by a student who has violated a classroom norm that is not explicitly stated ("The rules don't say I can't have a messy desk!"). For this reason, some teachers prefer to use a few general rules that encompass a host of possible concerns that may arise throughout the year. An example of a set of general rules might look like this

- ◆ Take care of yourself.
- ◆ Take care of each other.
- ◆ Take care of this place.

In the student situation discussed earlier, the teacher could cite the third rule as a reason for cleaning up the offending desk. For many teachers, a blend of both specific and general rules is the answer; there isn't a clear-cut advantage of using one kind over the other.

Brief and Positively Stated

In either case, the rules should be brief in number (three to five is advisable) and stated positively. Beware of a list of rules that all begin with the word, "No . . . " because these do not tell students what they should do, only what they should not do. Behavior cannot exist in a vacuum and in the absence of clearly stated rules students are left to speculate about what is acceptable.

Post the Rules

Once the rules have been developed, they should be clearly posted in the classroom. Young children may also benefit from picture symbols to represent each rule. Posted rules also allow visitors to the classroom and substitute teachers to reinforce the expectations for the class. Another advantage is that you can refer directly to the rule when redirecting a student's problem behavior.

Teach and Rehearse the Rules

As stated earlier, this is a critical component for ensuring an efficient classroom. The rules should be taught several times a day during the first week of school and revisited occasionally throughout the remainder of the year, especially after school breaks. The teacher should model each rule so that students can learn what they look and sound like. For example, if one of the rules is to take care of each other, the teacher can model examples of how students should speak to each other in class and on the playground. Non-examples are also useful, but be sure you do not ask a student to model a non-example, as you don't want to reinforce problem behavior.

Now You Try It

Draft a set of rules that might be useful for your classroom. Consider the developmental level of your students so that the rules reflect language that is meaningful to them. Remember to limit to about five rules overall, and be sure they are positively stated. Discuss your draft rules with a colleague to get constructive feedback. Once you have determined what your rules will be, post them in a place in your room where your students can see them and where you can easily refer to them.

References

Emmer, E., Evertson, C., & Anderson, L. (1980). Effective classroom management at the beginning of the school year. *Elementary School Journal, 80,* 219–231.

Evertson, C., & Emmer, E. (1982). Effective management at the beginning of the school year in junior high classes. *Journal of Educational Psychology, 74,* 485–498.

Kohn, A. (1996). *Beyond discipline: From compliance to community.* Alexandria, VA: Association for Supervision and Curriculum Development.

Matsumura, L. C., Slater, S. C., & Crosson, A. (2008). Classroom climate, rigorous instruction and curriculum, and students' interactions in urban middle schools. *Elementary School Journal, 108*(4), 293–312.

Rosenthal, R. (1974). *On the social psychology of the self-fulfilling prophecy: Further evidence of the Pygmalion effects and their medicating mechanisms.* New York: MSS Modular.

Staarman, J. K. (2009). The joint negotiation of ground rules: Establishing a shared collaborative practice with new educational technology. *Language and Education, 23*(1), 79-95.

Wong, H. K., & Wong, R. T. (2009). *The first days of school.* Mountain View, CA: Harry K. Wong.

8

Responding to Problem Behaviors

GRADE LEVELS: K–12

Time Needed: Several class sessions

What Is It?

Student behavior, indeed human behavior, is motivated by any one of several intentions. These intentions are meant to be communicative; that is, a set of behaviors is meant to signal to others what is needed. Adults tend to have a large repertoire of behaviors to signal what is needed. Clearing your throat is a somewhat subtle way of gaining a person's attention, but you have to admit that slapping someone will get their full attention even faster. However, as adults we have learned that it is not necessary to slap the person in front of you in the line at the grocery store to move up; a throat-clearing will usually do the trick.

This is all to say that we communicate with each other using myriad behaviors that signal others about what we want and need. These are not fully under our conscious control, and what we have learned to be effective has been shaped over the years by the feedback we get from others. Much of the behaviors we all engage in are motivated by one of four intentions: a need for attention, a desire for avoidance, to exert power, or to seek revenge (Kvols & Riedler, 1997). When considered in this light, the outward behaviors you observe take on a different meaning. Holding a sidebar conversation in class may be an attention-seeking behavior (either the peer's attention or yours), or it could be an avoidance behavior. Your responses to problem behaviors should be shaped by what you believe the student's intention is, even though he or she may rarely be able to say so him- or herself. Another way of gauging possible intent is to take note of your own response to the problem behavior. As a rule, attention-seeking and avoidance behaviors tend to elicit annoyance and low-level feelings with us; those problem behaviors motivated by revenge or power often elicit a stronger response on our part (Kvols & Riedler, 1997).

What Do I Do?

How do you determine what will occur when a rule is violated? This is perhaps the trickiest part of your classroom management plan because you don't want to find yourself writing a virtual law book of "if–then" scenarios. It's also not advisable to create a hierarchy of interventions that force you and the student to escalate the situation to increasingly more alarming levels. Many teachers have witnessed such a scenario, especially with older students, who are willing to "test drive" your rules to see just how far you'll take it. Instead of listing all the if–thens, give yourself the latitude to make more nuanced decisions about the problem behavior within context. A decision-making matrix of when to intercede is far more useful. Grossman advises intervening when any of these situations occur (2004, p. 276):

- **Harmful behavior.** When someone is likely to be injured physically or emotionally, or when something may be destroyed, an intervention by the teacher is required.
- **Distracting behavior.** If the behavior is interfering with the learning of others, you must intercede.
- **Testing behavior.** A student may test the system to see whether you will follow through. Needless to say, you must follow through.
- **Contagious behavior.** Some disruptive behaviors can spread through a classroom like wildfire. It is best to intervene before a number of students are involved.
- **Consistent behavior.** If the student has exhibited a pattern of misbehavior, it is necessary to develop a consistent response to the misbehavior.

Consider the Role of Timing in Your Response

A problem behavior does not always warrant an immediate response. Indeed, some are best left to be dealt with later. Grossman suggests these considerations when deciding when to respond (2004, p. 278):

- **Immediate response.** If the misbehavior is harmful, disruptive, or likely to be contagious, it is best to deal with it as soon as possible. These types of misbehavior can escalate quickly and become more serious.
- **Delayed response.** Sometimes you may not have all the facts, as when one student tattles on another. In this circumstance, it is better to delay your response until after you have been able to investigate. Other situations may warrant a delayed response because the timing is just not right. For example, if a student is very upset, or if your intervention will embarrass the student in front of peers, it may be better to wait until you can speak to the student privately.

This is especially true of older students, who can be made to feel as though they are losing face in the eyes of their peers. Don't put yourself or the student in a corner by forcing further problem behavior and escalating the situation. The goal always is to return the student to a learning state as rapidly as possible.

Have a Repertoire of Responses

Many effective teachers find that developing a toolkit of discipline procedures allows them the flexibility to make sound judgments regarding the nature of the situation. In all cases, the goal is to reengage the student in the learning situation as quickly as possible, not to mete out punishments or prove that you were the right one in the situation.

Repertoire of Responses

- **Move closer.** Proximity control works wonders for low-level behaviors. Often the presence of the teacher is enough to get a student back on task.

- **Signal.** A look, gesture, or pause can be an effective tool for ending a problem behavior. These signals should be quiet and meant for a single student.

- **Redirect.** Speak quietly to the student and restate what it is he or she should be doing. It's often effective to move close to the student, deliver the redirection, and then move away to allow him or her the opportunity to do so.

- **Replace.** Look for a competing behavior that makes the misbehavior impossible to complete. For example, a student cannot daydream when he or she has been given the task of distributing papers to the class.

- **Reduce.** Some problem behaviors can be minimized by reducing the task demand. A student who is having difficulty getting started on an assignment can benefit from having the task "chunked" into smaller segments. Tell the student to do the first question and promise to check in with him or her when he or she completes it. This can build momentum as well as student confidence in his or her ability to complete the task.

- **Relocate.** If the environment seems to be contributing to the misbehavior, relocate the student. Some learners are distracted by the conversations of others and may work better in a quiet location. As well, two students who have had a verbal or physical altercation need to be separated until emotions have calmed.

- **Ignore.** Not every problem behavior needs to be attended. If it does not meet any of the criteria listed (harmful, distracting, etc.), it may be one that should be ignored.

References

Grossman, H. (2004). *Classroom behavior management for diverse and inclusive schools* (3rd ed.). Lanham, MD: Rowman & Littlefield.

Kvols, K. J., & Riedler, B. (1997). *Redirecting children's misbehavior* (3rd ed.). Seattle, WA: Parenting Press.

9

De-escalating Problem Behaviors with Voluntary Removal

GRADE LEVELS: K–12

Time Needed: 1 hour

What Is It?

It should be anticipated that problem behaviors will arise, and that an effective teacher has tools at his or her disposal to respond to these situations. In elementary school, problem behaviors that are not resolved using techniques such as those in Chapter 8 are then reduced using a time-out procedure. Time out is the practice of removing a child from positive reinforcement for a prescribed number of minutes (Wolf, Risley, & Mees, 1964). This is usually accomplished by placing the child in a specific chair for punishment. The intent of time-out is to foster compliance, although others criticize the damaging effects on the caring relationship between teacher and student (Kohn, 1996; Paley, 1993). In addition, many teachers do not like to have their primary role redefined from educator to enforcer. The chill-out corner is an alternative to using time-out to alter student behavior. Unlike time-out, the chill-out corner is a comfortable space where a child who is upset can choose to go until he or she is feeling better.

The use of temporary, voluntary removal is useful for many students who are facing a difficulty and don't know how to resolve it. Many adults use this strategy in their own lives, choosing to "walk it off" rather than engage in hurtful or destructive behavior. However, a student rarely is given the opportunity to self-initiate a break outside of the classroom, and this confinement can inadvertently escalate a problem. The idea with a chill-out corner of the classroom is that a student can retreat to an emotionally and psychologically safe space to regroup. The availability and use of a voluntary removal also reinforces a student's self-regulatory behaviors, which are a critical life skill. As students recognize and acknowledge their frustration and then have a means to de-escalate themselves, they become more resilient in dealing with setbacks.

What Do I Do?

Determine where a quiet space can be created in your classroom. It should be away from the main traffic areas and offer a calm retreat from the bustle of the class. Some teachers place a beanbag chair or several large floor pillows in the area. In classrooms with older students, a cubby desk (one that has three vertical sides to shield visual stimulation) works well.

The next step is introducing the chill-out chair to students. Read Judith Viorst's *Alexander and the Terrible, Horrible, No Good, Very Bad Day* (1987) to the class to begin the discussion about what a person can do when he or she is feeling angry, hurt, or frustrated. In this picture book, Alexander states repeatedly that he is "going to Australia" because that sounds far removed from his troubles. Some teachers even label the chill-out corner "Australia" and decorate it with koala bears and kangaroos. Don't dismiss this book as being too elementary for older students. I have successfully used this (with more humor) with high school students who recall it from their own childhood and readily acknowledge that being able to settle down oneself is a mark of maturity. I hang posters of Australia inside the cubby desk when I am teaching older students.

As with all teaching, the chill-out corner works best when its use is modeled. Use role play to enact scenarios when a person might avail him- or herself of the corner, and even use it yourself a few times so that students begin to understand that it is not a punishment, but rather a good place to gather your thoughts. You may find that the corner is overused in the first few weeks, but this will correct itself as the novelty wears off. In the meantime, students learn a valuable lesson about the importance of self-regulation and autonomy.

Now You Try It

Call it whatever you like, but add the chill-out corner to your room arrangement map and detail its use in your classroom management plan in the discipline section. After introducing the corner to your students, use other children's literature that illustrates difficult behavior in childhood. The books in the box below can be used as read-alouds to prompt constructive conversations.

> ### Literature Connections
>
> Bang, M. G. (1999). *When Sophie gets angry—really, really, angry.* New York: Scholastic.
>
> Gilmore, R. (2001). *A screaming kind of day.* Ontario, Canada: Fitzhenry & Whiteside.
>
> Sendak, M. (1988). *Where the wild things are.* New York: HarperCollins.
>
> Shannon, D. (1998). *No David!* New York: Scholastic.
>
> Shannon, D. (1999). *David goes to school.* New York: Blue Sky.
>
> Viorst, J. (1987). *Alexander and the terrible, horrible, no good, very bad day.* New York: Aladdin.

References

Kohn, A. (1996). *Beyond discipline: From compliance to community.* Alexandria, VA: Association for Supervision and Curriculum Development.

Paley, V. G. (1993). *You can't say you can't play.* Cambridge, MA: Harvard University Press.

Wolf, M., Risley, T., & Mees, H. (1964). Application of operant conditioning procedures to the behavior problems of an autistic child. *Behaviour Research and Therapy, 1,* 305–312.

10

Crumple Doll

GRADE LEVELS: K–3

Time Needed: 15 minutes

What Is It?

Name-calling is the most common kind of verbal aggression in schools. Children and adults often accept this practice as part of the expected exchange of young children without fully appreciating the lasting effects it can have on people. A student of student aggression found that girls were more likely to use name-calling as a tool for rejection from social circles (Schuster, 1996).

What Do I Do?

Young children need to learn empathy to prevent name-calling and teasing. An instructional activity to promote empathetic understanding is the Crumple Doll (Katz, Sax, & Fisher, 2003). Cut a paper doll out of a brown shopping bag (it will look at bit like a gingerbread man). Tell students that the paper doll represents a child their age at another school. Explain that this child is called names by her classmates, like "stupid" and "ugly." With each name, crumple a part of the doll until it is in a small ball. Invite students to brainstorm what kinds of words the paper doll would need to hear in order to return to her former shape. Students will invariably conclude that kind words will restore the paper doll. As they give examples of kind words, begin to smooth it out. When the paper doll has been unfolded, show the students that the wrinkles still remain. Remind them that cruel words remain inside a person for a long time. At the conclusion of the lesson, hang the crumple doll in a prominent place as a reminder of the effects of name-calling. If you overhear an incidence of name-calling in the classroom, walk over to the paper doll and crumple a part of it. This serves as a dramatic cue about the power of words.

Now You Try It

Observe your students on the playground, in the cafeteria, and in the hallways for incidences of name-calling. Identify the frequency and types of taunting that occur most frequently and tailor your Crumple Doll story to make it meaningful for your students. Use this lesson as an introduction of books featuring name-calling. While some of the books in the box below have been mentioned in other sections, their story lines lend themselves to name-calling discussions with your class.

Name-Calling Books

dePaola, T. (1979). *Oliver Button is a sissy*. New York: Harcourt Brace.

Estes, E. (1944). *The hundred dresses*. San Diego, CA: Harcourt Brace.

Havill, J. (1989). *Jamaica tag-along*. Boston: Houghton Mifflin.

Henkes, K. (1991). *Chrysanthemum*. New York: Mulberry.

Hoberman, M. A. (1999). *And to think that we thought we'd never be friends*. New York: Crown.

Lester, H. (1999). *Hooway for Wodney Wat*. New York: Houghton Mifflin.

Shannon, D. (1999). *A bad case of stripes*. New York: Scholastic.

Whitcomb, M. E. (1998). *Odd Velvet*. San Francisco: Chronicle.

Wood, A. (1988). *Elbert's bad word*. San Diego, CA: Harcourt Brace.

References

Katz, L., Sax, C., & Fisher, D. (2003). *Activities for a diverse classroom: Connecting students* (2nd ed.). Colorado Springs, CO: PEAK Parent Center.

Schuster, B. (1996). Mobbing, bullying, and peer rejection. *Psychological Science Agenda*, July/August, 12–13.

11

Responding to Bullying

GRADE LEVELS: K–6

Time Needed: 30 minutes to hours

What Is It?

Teasing and name-calling are the most common forms of verbal aggression in schools (Shakeshaft, 1997). Despite acknowledgment that this is a form of bullying, many adults regard it as a normal—even necessary—part of childhood (Olweus, 1991). Bullying can undermine the classroom community and is perceived as acceptable when the teacher does little to respond to it.

What Do I Do?

The most effective response a teacher can offer is a proactive one. Preventative steps can include:

◆ **Establish a classroom rule.** The playground is the harshest environment for some children, especially those who are seen as outsiders by others. Left unchecked, children will exclude one another from play, often hurling uncharitable words in the process. A rule authored in partnership with the class can eliminate such interactions. This rule may be worded as "Everyone here can play" (Paley, 1992; Sapon-Shevin, Dobbelaere, Corrigan, Goodman, & Mastin, 1998). The intent of this rule is to eliminate exclusion by requiring students to create a way for a classmate to join a group at play, rather that simply telling the child "You can't play with us." Once the rule is established, children will need many opportunities to practice using it. This should be modeled by the teacher and praised when witnessed.

◆ **Use children's literature within the curriculum.** A number of excellent books have been written on the subject of bullying and are listed at the end of this section (Frey, 2002). The titles in the box below are useful for promoting discussion of this topic.

Books with Bullying Themes

Carlson, N. L. (1997). *How to lose all your friends.* New York: Puffin.

Cohen-Posey, K. (1995). *How to handle bullies, teasers, and other meanies: A book that takes the nuisance out of name calling and other nonsense.* Highland City, FL: Rainbow.

Hoose, P. (1998). *Hey little ant.* Berkeley, CA: Tricycle.

McCain, B. R. (2001). *Nobody knew what to do: A story about bullying.* New York: Albert Whitman.

Naylor, P. R. (1994). *King of the playground.* New York: Aladdin.

O'Neill, A. (2002). *The recess queen.* New York: Scholastic.

Romain, T. (1998). *Cliques, phonies, and other baloney.* Minneapolis, MN: Free Spirit.

◆ **Teach students how to protect themselves against being victimized.** The research on bullying has progressed significantly in the last decade. In particular, it is now understood that a bullying incident involves not only the two primary parties, but also witnesses and bystanders. In addition, it is also understood that students who are habitually bullied often exhibit certain behaviors that make them likely targets. Chief among these is isolation from other peers—a student who is socially isolated is more likely to be bullied. The Colorado Anti-Bullying Project (*www.no-bully.com*) reminds students to "STAMP out bullying" using this mnemonic:

> **S**tay away from bullies.
> **T**ell someone when it takes place.
> **A**void bad situations.
> **M**ake friends.
> **P**roject confidence.

◆ This advice is necessary for bystanders and witnesses, too. A bullying event is often a complex interaction that can be fueled by an audience. Those who stand by silently, as well as those who encourage the bullying but do not directly participate, play a role in the event.

◆ **Create a forum for students to resolve disputes.** The establishment of a peace table can provide children with both the space and the structure to resolve problems in a constructive manner. See the next chapter in this book for a more detailed explanation of the Peace Table.

Even with a proactive approach, bullying issues can still arise. Again, the eyes of your students are on you. View this as an opportunity to teach, not just a problem to solve.

♦ **Meet with both parties separately.** There are issues to address on both sides. Each student needs to hear directly from you about the problem and the solution.

♦ **Notify the families so they can collaborate with you.** Don't hesitate to consult with the families to solve the problem. They are often the source of the best ideas for working effectively with their child.

♦ **Get the school administration involved.** Incidents of bullying can rapidly spiral into very serious situations. Make sure an administrator and a counselor are involved in solving bullying problems that do not respond to classroom interventions.

Now You Try It

Are any of the marginalized students you have identified in your classroom being bullied or are they bullies themselves? Don't just look for evidence of physical intimidation. Most bullying events are relational in nature, and are typically targeted at excluding a particular student. Take a look at the student's cumulative file, and ask questions of the school counselor and previous teachers. Whether the student is a victim of bullying, or is targeting another student through exclusion or intimidation, that student needs the support and intervention that comes from a caring school community. When a bullying event occurs, who are the witnesses and bystanders? All of these parties need to be a part of the resolution of the situation.

References

Colorado Anti-bullying project. (n.d.). STAMP out bullying. Retrieved from *www.no-bully.com*.

Frey, N. (2002). What's in a name? Honoring students' experiences and perspectives. *Dragon Lode, 21*(1), 1–6.

Olweus, D. (1991). Bully/victim problems among schoolchildren: Some basic facts and effects of a school-based intervention program. In D. Pepler & K. Rubin (Eds.), *The development and treatment of childhood aggression* (pp. 411–448). Hillsdale, NJ: Erlbaum.

Paley, V. G. (1992). *You can't say you can't play.* Cambridge, MA: Harvard University Press.

Sapon-Shevin, M., Dobbelaere, A., Corrigan, C., Goodman, K., & Mastin, M. (1998). Everyone here can play. *Educational Leadership, 56*(1), 42–45.

Shakeshaft, C. (1997). Boys call me cow. *Educational Leadership, 55*(2), 22–25.

12

Fostering Problem Solving among Students

GRADE LEVELS: K–6

Time Needed: 30 minutes

What Is It?

Students need to take part in the resolution of problems and not merely rely upon adults to solve them. However, children need the support of caring adults to teach them the skills they need to resolve these problems. While secondary students typically have peer conflict–resolution programs at their schools, most elementary schools do not. This reinforces a "tattletale" method among students, who feel compelled to report to the teacher and then await the dispensation of justice. All of this, of course, is quite exhausting to the teacher, who is often left to resolve the small conflicts that arise in class and on the playground. A solution is to create a forum for resolving disputes.

Conflicts between students occur in the classroom, on the playground, and before and after school. Unfortunately, a teacher unprepared to deal with these disputes is placed in the unenviable position of trying to figure out what happened. Rather than playing judge and jury in a disagreement, it is preferable to teach conflict–resolution skills (Porro, 1996). The peace table is a forum for settling quarrels and provides a healthy outlet for students to state their position and listen to others.

What Do I Do?

All students should be taught how to resolve disputes when they arise. These steps can serve children well when an argument flares up.

1 When you feel yourself becoming angry, find a way to calm yourself down by leaving the argument or counting to five before saying anything.

2 Use an I-statement to explain how you're feeling ("When you _____, I felt _____. I would like for you to _____.").

3 Listen to what the other person has to say.

4 Discuss the problem calmly until you arrive at a solution both of you can agree upon.

5 If you cannot agree, ask the teacher for a meeting at the peace table.

The peace table should be situated in a quiet spot in the room for students to discuss their dispute with some privacy. Before coming to the peace table, each student should take some time to collect his or her thoughts using Form 12.1 at the end of this chapter. You will want to mediate these conversations during the first weeks of school until you are comfortable with the students' skill at handling this on their own. When sitting in on a peace table conversation, avoid actively participating and offer guidance only on the process, not the outcome.

Now You Try It

Decide where you will locate your peace table and add this to your room arrangement and classroom management plan. It is important to include discussion of the peace table in your letter to families. You can reinforce the steps of conflict–resolution in your classroom through modeling and by reading and discussing children's literature on disputes, including the titles in the box below.

> ### Books with Conflict–Resolution Themes
>
> Hawkes, K. (2003). *And to think that we thought we'd never be friends.* New York: Dragonfly.
> Munson, D. (2000). *Enemy pie.* San Francisco: Chronicle.

Reference

Porro, B. (1996). *Talk it out: Conflict resolution in the elementary classroom.* Alexandria, VA: Association for Supervision and Curriculum Development.

FORM 12.1

Form for a Peace Table

Before your meeting at the peace table:

What is your name? _____

What is the name of the other person? _____

What do you believe the disagreement is about? _____

_____

_____

_____

Write an I-statement that explains the way *you* feel.

When you _____

I felt _____.

I would like _____

_____

_____

Write an I-statement you believe the *other person* might say.

When you _____

I felt _____.

I would like _____

_____

_____

After your meeting at the peace table:

What did both of you agree to do? _____

_____

_____

_____

_____

_____

_____

_____

13

Room Arrangement

GRADE LEVELS: K–12

Time Needed: Several hours

What Is It?

Educational researchers define the learning environment as both a social one and a physical one. In the previous part, you aimed your attention at the social environment, especially as it relates to management and learning. However, the physical environment of your classroom also contributes greatly to your students' ability to learn. Without realizing it, students make a number of judgments about you and themselves based on the physical environment. Is it organized and neat? So is my teacher. Are there interesting items on display for me to use? This is my classroom and I belong here. Emmer, Evertson, and Worsham (2002) advise teachers to consider visibility, proximity, accessibility, and safety when arranging a classroom. Because each classroom is unique, the arrangement you decide on will be influenced by your academic needs and by student considerations. Keep in mind that students with disabilities may have learning needs that necessitate particular placement in the classroom to increase visibility or minimize distractions.

What Do I Do?

Students need to be able to hear, see, and move around the room in order to engage in the many learning opportunities in your classroom. A failure to attend to these issues can result in learning difficulties for individual students. In addition, your activity in the classroom must also be considered. You need to easily access materials, work with individual students, engage in small-group discussions, and display information. Use these guiding questions to develop a room arrangement that works well for you and your students.

Visibility

Are there areas of the classroom where students cannot easily view the board or screen? If so, consider using these areas for other purposes, including small-group work or storage.

Proximity

Proximity is the physical distance between you and a student and is a useful tool for increasing student engagement. Look at the pathways for teacher movement in your classroom. Can you easily reach each student in the room to provide extra instructional or behavioral support? Can you circulate during whole-group teaching to monitor learning? Jones (2007) suggests that you arrange student desks to provide both an interior loop and an exterior loop to use around the classroom (see Figure 13.1). This gives you proximity to all the students in your class and decreases off-task behavior. Keep proximity between students in mind as well. Engaging classrooms use partner arrangements throughout the day. Be certain that students can easily move into partner groups at your direction. For more information on partnering, see Part Four.

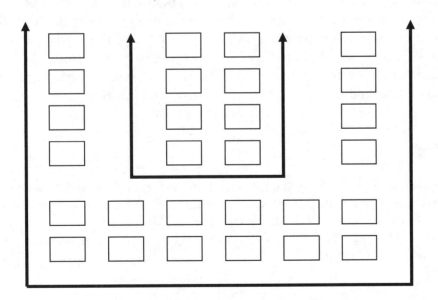

FIGURE 13.1. Room arrangement.

Accessibility

An orderly learning environment allows for students to easily reach materials and areas of the classroom. Students need to sharpen pencils, throw away trash, enter and exit the room, and choose books from the classroom library. How will this be accomplished in your room? When planning your room arrangement, consider patterns of movement in these high-traffic areas. For example, teachers routinely locate the wastebasket next to their desk, despite the fact that nearly all the users should not be near the desk. Instead, place the wastebasket in an area of the room that is convenient for students and does not bring them near your desk, where confidential materials are easily accessible.

Safety

Above all, students must be safe in your classroom. All schools have specific requirements for maintaining unobstructed exits in case of fire. Be sure to consult these regulations when planning your room arrangement. Next, catalog the items that may pose a threat to student safety. Is there science lab equipment stored in your classroom? If so, this should be placed in a secure area.

Now You Try It

Measure your classroom space and map it onto graph paper. Be sure to note windows, doors, electrical outlets, computer stations, and other fixed objects. Cut out scaled shapes of the furniture you have available in your room and place them on the graph paper. Pay attention to visibility, proximity, accessibility, and safety concerns. This can also be accomplished digitally. Use the Classroom Architect tool at *classroom.4teachers.org* to set the dimensions of your classroom, place furniture and storage, and experiment with alternative arrangements.

References

4teachers.org. (n.d.). Classroom architect. Retrieved from *classroom.4teachers.org*.

Emmer, E. T., Evertson, C. M., & Worsham, M. E. (2002). *Classroom management for secondary teachers* (6th ed.). Boston: Pearson Allyn & Bacon.

Jones, F. H. (2007). *Fred Jones tools for teaching: Discipline, instruction, motivation* (2nd ed.). Santa Cruz, CA: Author.

14

Taking Attendance

GRADE LEVELS: K–12

Time Needed: Less than 5 minutes

What Is It?

Taking daily attendance is one of the many clerical responsibilities of classroom teachers. Absences, tardy students, and attendance must be reported accurately and in a timely fashion in order to fulfill the legal obligations of the school. In addition, student safety is a consideration, especially when students fail to appear for school. Schools are *in loco parentis*, a legal term that means the school assumes the supervisory responsibilities of a child during school hours. In addition, schools are funded by the state based on average daily attendance (ADA). Accurate records of attendance are required by law, and failure to do so can result in lost income for the school.

Accurate attendance records are also needed for day-to-day management of the class. Taking attendance conveys to students that they are expected and that their presence is necessary. In addition, the attendance difficulties of an individual student are a signal for intervention. There may be a pattern to the absences; for example, a child is routinely absent on days when a physical education class takes place. A parent conference is in order for chronic absences, and there may be more serious consequences involving other agencies. These circumstances demand an accurate and complete account of a student's attendance.

What Do I Do?

Collection of daily attendance is usually done at the beginning of the school day or class session. However, this occurs precisely at one of the busiest times of the school day: a child needs assistance with belongings, a student worker is at the door to deliver a note from the office, and an impatient parent is waiting in the hallway to speak with you. In the meantime, students may be wandering around the room. You need a system for gathering attendance information quickly and accurately. Here are several ideas for collecting attendance.

◆ **Use bellwork to create a quiet time at the beginning of class.** An effective way to establish an orderly environment at the beginning of class is to use the daily practice of bellwork, a prompt or question posted on the board as students arrive. Because they have been taught this procedure, students know they are to begin writing a response as soon as they are in their seat. Teachers typically instruct students to write until the bell or timer rings for class to begin. Bellwork prompts can be as simple or complex as you decide.

> "What did you have for dinner last night? Was it a favorite?"
> "Write about a time when you were able to surprise someone."
> "Yesterday we discussed the confederacy's reasons for declaring war on the United States. What do you believe were the arguments for and against such an action in Southern newspapers?"

◆ While students are writing, you have an ideal opportunity to record attendance data and attend to any other immediate details that cannot wait. Another advantage to bellwork is the way it activates students' thinking to prepare them for your content. Further strategies for bellwork can be found in Part Five of this book.

◆ **Engage students in the process of taking their own attendance.** Very young children may have difficulty with writing a bellwork response. Another means for gathering attendance and student information is by posting a chart each morning with a question on it. As students arrive, they answer the question by choosing a wooden clothespin with their name written on the side and affixing it to the proper column. For example, lunch counts are required daily in some schools to determine how many students can be expected to purchase lunch. The teacher can laminate a chart with "Buy My Lunch" and a photograph on one side and "Bring My Lunch" on the other. Students fasten their lunch clip in the appropriate column. At a glance the teacher has both lunch count and attendance information because absent students' clothespins remain in the container. See Figure 14.1 for an example of such a chart.

◆ **Appoint a student monitor.** Gathering attendance information can be assigned to a student each week. Classroom jobs like these can be assigned using a chart of such duties. Students can read the chart to find out what their assignment is for

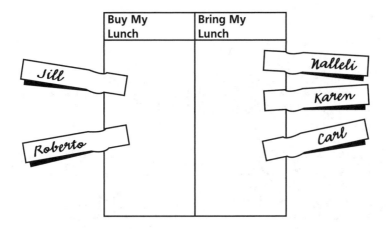

FIGURE 14.1. Attendance and lunch chart with clothespins.

the week. The attendance monitor completes an attendance grid each morning and gives it to the teacher. Since attendance forms are a legal document, the teacher must verify the accuracy of the information before signing the form.

♦ **Use assigned seats and a seating chart.** This is especially effective during the first weeks of school because you can quickly scan the classroom to locate the names of students who are absent. Keep a reproducible chart handy to record changes in seat assignments.

Now You Try It

Decide how you will take attendance in your classroom and add it to your notes for developing your classroom management plan. It is important to have a procedure in place so that the task of collecting attendance information does not interfere with the level of student engagement in your classroom. Be sure to consult the school and district policies on taking attendance. In many schools, attendance is collected electronically via a student database management system. These can be initially tricky to navigate, so if you are unsure of how to do so, ask a mentor teacher or administrator. Taking attendance has many ramifications for a school, and they will not regard your request for assistance as trivial.

15

What to Do When a Student Returns from an Absence

GRADE LEVELS: K–12

Time Needed: 1–10 minutes

What Is It?

Throughout the school year students will be absent from school due to illness, family emergency, or travel. At times these are unavoidable, while at other times they are planned in advance. However, absences from school have far-flung effects beyond the days and weeks following. One large-scale study found that the number of absences a child had in fourth grade was a strong predictor of passage of a high-stakes graduation exam administered six years later (Zau & Betts, 2008). The problem, of course, is missed instruction, and a high number of absences risks leaving the child further and further behind his or her peers. To be sure, attendance is influenced in part by a child's health and socioeconomic status (Furstenberg, Waller, & Wang, 2003). As with the behavioral supports discussed earlier in this part, the teacher's goal is always to return the student to a learning state as quickly as possible. This is especially true for students who have been absent from instruction, as they are likely to be behind their classmates in their assignments and learning.

What Do I Do?

The return of a student to the classroom can pose a disruption for the teacher because he or she must take time from instruction to inform the learner about what he or she has missed. In addition, the wait the other students must endure results in more lost instructional time. Several procedures can be put into place in your classroom to ensure that students receive materials and assignment information for days missed.

♦ **When an absence is planned, have a contract ready for students to complete work while gone from school.** It is not uncommon for students to be absent for non-health-related reasons, such as visiting another place. In some communities, families proactively seek work from the teacher in advance of a trip. However, a responsive classroom should not be completely dependent on the parent to initiate contact. Listen to classroom conversations and ask your student when you hear of a possible upcoming absence. Prepare real work, not busy work, for the student to complete. Pertinent readings and assignments are far more useful than a packet of worksheets haphazardly thrown together. Outline these in a contract with the student and family and collect and grade it when the student returns. In some cases, the location may be of particular interest academically. Work with the student and family to assign meaningful work that takes the context of the trip into consideration. For example, sixth-grade student, Gregory, regularly posted on his classroom's blog while he traveled with his family to Egypt.

♦ **Establish an absence notebook for gathering information.** Most absences are not planned and are often health related. An absence notebook is an efficient method for keeping track of materials a student will need when he or she returns. The student who is charged with attendance duties for the week can also maintain the notebook. Whenever handouts and informational flyers are distributed, the attendance monitor gathers extra copies for those who are absent. In addition, they note assignments and due dates on a log kept in the notebook. A blank version of this log appears in Form 15.1 at the end of this chapter. When the absent student returns, he or she can go to the notebook to collect materials and assignment information missed. The notebook is also useful for students who were present but may have forgotten some important information.

♦ **Assign a scribe for note taking.** Many teachers require students to take notes during lectures. These lecture notes are useful when students complete homework and review for a test. To ensure that absent students have access to missed lectures, keep a box of carbon paper on hand for days when a student is absent. Ask a classmate to slip a piece of carbon paper between a notebook page and a sheet of loose-leaf paper to generate an identical copy of his or her notes. These carbon copies should be placed in the absence notebook at the end of class. Remember that a sheet of carbon paper can be used many times before it must be discarded. This is also an effective accommodation for a student with a disability who cannot generate his or her own notes.

Teachers of secondary school students often use PowerPoint slides to augment their teaching. Post these slides routinely on your classroom website or e-platform so that students and families can access them. This will also provide students who have not been absent with additional tools to use for review as they study for tests and exams. In addition, they serve as a record of the curriculum and instruction for the course and are useful for reviews before state tests.

♦ **Create assignment partners.** Assignment partners are pairs of students who have been assigned the task of providing information for each other. Each student serves as a point of contact for the other to clarify information about homework and assignments. The assignment partner can also meet with the returning student to review details of the assignments for class. Because this is meant to be a peer-support strategy, it is best to assign partners rather than allow students to choose. This eliminates the possibility of hurt feelings at being left out and encourages students to communicate with fellow classmates who are not in their social network. Further details about assignment partners appear in Chapter 31.

♦ **Schedule time for returning students to meet with you.** During the rush of the day it is easy to forget about the child who has returned from an absence. Establish a routine in your schedule, perhaps near the end of the class or school day, for returning students to consult with you about things they have missed. Students should be reminded that they must first pick up their assignments from the absence notebook and meet with their assignment partner.

Now You Try It

Familiarize yourself with your school district's policy on student absences. After adding this information to your classroom management plan, outline your procedures for dealing with student absences in your class. If you have a classroom website, or if your school uses an e-platform for courses, create a place where previously taught lesson materials are held. Be sure to let both students and their family know how to access them.

References

Furstenberg, F. F., Waller, M. R., & Wang, H. (2003). *The well-being of California's children*. San Francisco: Public Policy Institute of California.

Zau, A. C., & Betts, J. R. (2008). *Predicting success, preventing failure: An investigation of the California high school exit exam*. San Francisco: Public Policy Institute of California.

Log for Absence Notebook

While You Were Out

Here is a list of this week's assignments. Be sure to copy them into your assignment notebook.

Date	Assignment	Details you should know	Due date	Whom to ask for extra help

Engaging Students through Organization

16

Posting a Daily Schedule

GRADE LEVELS: K–12

Time Needed: 5 minutes to post and review

What Is It?

A daily schedule serves as a visual organizer for students entering the classroom. The schedule should list the major learning events of the day in chronological order and may also include times. The consistent use of a posted schedule establishes a predictable learning environment and assists learners in pacing their rate of work. A daily schedule is particularly useful for students who have difficulty transitioning from one task to another (Wien, 1996). The use of a visual daily schedule is recommended for some students with disabilities, especially those with communication difficulties, or with autism (Banda, Grimmett, & Hart, 2009). Posted daily schedules are an excellent support for some students with disabilities who may require more structure. Students who are ELLs can also benefit from schedules that are paired with pictures.

A posted daily schedule is commonly used in classrooms for younger students, as well as those that have members with IEPs. However, the usefulness of this is not limited to those populations.

What Do I Do?

Realia Schedules

The schedule should be meaningful to the students using it. Therefore, the structure of the daily schedule is directly influenced by the language development of the students. The most concrete form is a realia schedule, which features the actual object as a symbol for the activity. This type of schedule, which relies on objects rather than words or pictures, is especially useful in preschool classrooms, as well as for students with cognitive or sensory disabilities that make text or visuals more difficult to discern or understand. For instance, a realia schedule in a primary classroom might include a picture book of the day's read-aloud, a pencil for journal writing, and a ball to represent recess.

Picture Schedules

Daily schedules can be augmented with simple pictures to symbolize the activity; for example, journal writing can be represented by a photograph or graphic of a pencil and paper. Snapshots of classmates performing the learning activity are also effective. A pocket-chart display makes it easy for you to change the schedule each day. This process is useful for students who are acquiring text-based literacy, as it pairs a written with a more familiar and accessible picture.

A separate schedule can be established for literacy and math centers in which students move through a series of small-group activities stationed around the classroom. To ensure students know what is expected, prepare individual cards with each student's name and place these cards next to the symbol for each center and display it in a pocket chart hung in a prominent area of the classroom. Students can consult the schedule to locate the correct center and at a glance you can monitor whether everyone is where they need to be.

Whiteboard

Students in intermediate and secondary classes can follow an agenda posted on the whiteboard. Use the same location each day so students can readily find the schedule. Your agenda should consist of the date to signal that it is current, and contain a brief description of the activity. You may decide to pair times with your agenda, but consider that this may cause problems for you if a particular activity takes longer than planned.

Now You Try It

Consider the oral and written language levels of the students in your class when choosing a format for your daily schedule. Keep in mind that individual support needs may necessitate the use of realia or pictures in addition to written information. Be sure that the schedule is updated each day (or each class) so that the information posted is current and accurate.

References

Banda, D. R., Grimmett, E., & Hart, S. (2009). Activity schedules: Helping students with autism spectrum disorders in general education classes manage transition issues. *Teaching Exceptional Children, 41*(4), 16–21.

Wien, C. A. (1996). Time, work, and developmentally appropriate practice. *Early Childhood Research Quarterly, 11*, 377–393.

17

Signaling the Class

GRADE LEVELS: K–12

Time Needed: Less than 30 seconds

What Is It?

Teachers need a signal to gain the attention of students at the beginning of class or when transitioning from one activity to another. The signal should be taught daily during the first week of school and reinforced frequently until students respond quickly and consistently. The use of a signal to gain attention promotes student engagement by minimizing the amount of lost instructional time. This last point deserves further attention. A study of first-grade classrooms found that teachers who spent time orienting students to the next activity required less time for the transition, and the students in these classrooms spent more time in child-directed learning activities, such as collaborative learning, than those in classrooms that did not use transition techniques (Cameron, Connor, & Morrison, 2005). In addition, smooth transitions minimize the behavioral difficulties that can arise. Students with behavioral disabilities are especially vulnerable to loosely managed transitions. In many cases they are blamed for the problem behavior, without consideration for the lack of environmental signals that could have prevented the difficulty from arising in the first place. Students who are new to English are also vulnerable to a lack of signals. When directions are only provided verbally, and are not paired with audible or gestural signals, they may miss the language-based directions and be unfairly viewed as being noncompliant.

What Do I Do?

The signal you select should be easy to use and easy for others to replicate. Some teachers like to use a bell to gain the attention of the class. While these sounds often carry well in the room, a disadvantage is that the bell must first be located in the classroom. If you are not standing near the bell, you must walk to another area of the room. This results in a delay. Flashing the light switch is not effective because it results in a startle response, rather than an attentive one. Remember that the signal you choose to teach should communicate what you want students to do.

It is preferable to have a consistent signal that combines a verbal command with a hand gesture. Once taught, these signals generalize well to other settings, such as the cafeteria, playground, and hallways. Signals should be developmentally appropriate and easy to remember. In the early weeks of school, these signals should be practiced frequently and augmented with a poster or other visual display. Remember to wait until you have everyone's attention before beginning the next activity.

1–2–3, Eyes on Me

This signal is best for primary classrooms. Students are taught that when this signal is given, they are to stop what they are doing, place their hands on their heads, and look at the teacher. For the youngest of children, you may have them respond, "1–2, eyes on you."

Stop–Look–Listen

Pair this verbal command with a series of hand signals.

- **"Stop."** Raise the palm of your hand in a 'stop' gesture.
- **"Look."** Point to your eyes.
- **"Listen."** Point to your ear.

If You Hear My Voice, _____

This is another signal appropriate for elementary classrooms. When you need to gain the attention of a busy classroom, announce, "If you hear my voice, clap once" and follow it with a single hand clap. "If you hear my voice, clap twice" and then do so. You will rarely need to get to three before all eyes are on you.

Give Me Five

Older students do not need to place their hands on their heads in order to demonstrate that they are giving the teacher their attention. However, you want them to exhibit some outward behaviors that convey their state of attention. This signal is delivered with a raised hand and symbolizes each step a student must cycle through to display full attention. Announce these while counting off with your fingers.

1   "Stop what you are doing."

2   "Mouth is quiet."

3   "Look at the teacher."

4   "Hands are still."

5   "Listen for directions."

Silent Hand Signal

This is similar to Give Me Five, but is performed silently. Teach your students that when you want their attention you will raise your hand. They are expected to look at you and raise their hand in response. In addition, each student has the responsibility of tapping on the shoulder of a neighbor who is not yet raising his or her hand.

Audible Tones

Many teachers rely on an audible tone produced by an object. There are many devices that can accomplish this including a bell, slide whistle, rain stick, or wooden rasp. If you use such signals, consider the relative noise level appropriate for the occasion. A slide whistle is too loud to signal the end of sustained silent reading, but perfect for notifying students that the end of the science lab is approaching. A rain stick, which has a gentle sound, is a better choice for the end of a quiet activity. Keep in mind that the purpose of such devices is to alert, not startle. Remember to pair the audible tone with a verbal direction so that students know what to do next.

Now You Try It

Decide what signal you will use and create a classroom poster to represent each step. Plan to teach this signal several times a day for the first week. Use this signal consistently so that it becomes a habit for you and your students. In addition, make sure to teach other personnel in your classroom (student teachers, visiting teachers) the signals you use in order to capitalize on your procedures for managing transitions.

Reference

Cameron, C. E., Connor, C. M., & Morrison, F. J. (2005). Effects of teacher organization on classroom functioning. *Journal of School Psychology, 43*(1), 61–85.

18

Monitoring Noise Level

GRADE LEVELS: K–6

Time Needed: Less than 30 seconds

What Is It?

Effective classrooms feature daily partner and small-group work. This can result in a noise level that may exceed your tolerance and interfere with the learning of other students. However, it is not efficient to announce every few minutes that students need to lower their voices. Instead, students need to learn what levels of noise are acceptable for a given learning activity. By teaching, rather than reprimanding, students learn to self-monitor.

The issue of self-regulation is an important one for students. As they progress through school, they are increasingly expected to make decisions based on the needs of the group, and to do so intrinsically. Older students who must rely on external reminders to regulate their behavior and actions are perceived as being problem students. However, relatively little attention is given to how the student might go about acquiring these skills. Classroom procedures that support the development of self-regulation are a useful bridge in fostering the skills needed when working within large and small groups.

What Do I Do?

Visual representations of noise levels provide students with immediate feedback so they can modulate their voices. The idea behind these approaches is that the pairing of a visual reminder with the sound of the classroom teaches students how to regulate their behavior. Be sure to teach through modeling and practice so students can learn about your expectations.

Noise Meter

Construct a simple dial out of cardboard or stiff paper like the one seen in Figure 18.1. Use a brass brad to attach an arrow to the dial so that you can move it as needed. Label each section and then have students practice using voice volumes appropriate for tests and reading, partner work, learning centers and small-group projects, and outdoor activities. During class, adjust the arrow on the dial to reflect the appropriate noise level. Some teachers construct a large version of the noise meter and prop it in the whiteboard tray so that it is readily accessible.

Traffic Signal

This is a version of the noise meter for younger children. Construct a traffic signal from construction paper. Before introducing an activity, practice using the voice volume appropriate for the task. Point to each light as you and the children use a variety of volumes. This is also useful for addressing problems associated with voice volumes that are too low, such as when speaking in front of the class.

Classroom Lights

This can be used for demonstration purposes in a classroom with lights on a dimmer switch. Model the voice levels for various classroom activities, adjusting the brightness to illustrate the relative volume you want students to use. If your classroom lights are not wired this way, use a lamp with a dimmer switch.

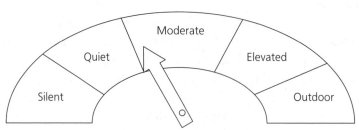

Silent—When we take a test
Quiet—When we read and work independently
Moderate—When we are working in learning centers
Elevated—When we are working in groups
Outdoor—On the playground

FIGURE 18.1. Noise meter.

Now You Try It

How is the noise level in your classroom? If your students are not skilled at modulating their voices to match the instructional activity, create a lesson for introducing volume. Consider using music and musical instruments as a means for introducing relative volume. The folk song "John Jacob Jingleheimer Schmidt" is a great piece of music for teaching about volume and the musical concept of dynamics. You will find that the need for formal devices for teaching self-monitoring of noise levels will decrease as the school year progresses, provided these have been carefully taught and consistently used in the fall.

Engaging Students through Organization

19

Reaching Students
to Manage Their Time

GRADE LEVELS: K–12

Time Needed: 1–5 minutes

What Is It?

Engaging classrooms offer students a variety of instructional arrangements throughout the day (Good & Brophy, 2003). The frequent movement of students from one activity to another requires that the teacher have procedures in place to minimize disruptions. Increasing a student's time on an academic task is directly linked to learning outcomes (Walberg, 1988). Therefore, effective educators use procedures that promote smooth transitions between classroom events. Once the new activity has been introduced, students are further challenged to use the allotted time wisely in order to complete the task. Many students struggle with how to best use their time to ensure completion of the activity. This is another aspect of self-regulation and can remain a challenge for older students who have repeatedly been told to pick up the pace, but have received little instruction in how to do so.

Strategies for transitions have appeared previously in this part, and are combined to provide smooth transitions. These include posting a schedule and using a method for signaling students to gain attention. A third component for transitions is defining the time allotted for movement. It is useful to provide a temporal boundary for the task so that the activity has an appropriate level of urgency. The pacing that is set for the transition lets your students know that learning is a priority and therefore not a minute is to be wasted.

Teachers sometimes wonder whether the pacing set for an activity or its transition can be overwhelming. Without doubt the transition should justly consider the demands of the activity. If there are many materials to cleaned, sorted, and put away, then the time allotted should reflect a reasonable expectation of how long this will take. On the other hand, if the transition involves only moving to another area of the classroom, little time is needed. An appropriately paced transition should not cause panicked movement, nor encourage a lackadaisical atmosphere. In addition, a time allotment that is paired by elapsed time provides students with experience at managing and self-regulating their time.

What Do I Do?

Chalkboard Countdown

Students working in small groups need assistance in monitoring their pacing in order to complete the assigned tasks. A simple way to accomplish this is by using a chalkboard countdown. When giving students directions about the learning task, discuss time allotment. Post a descending series of numbers to indicate the number of minutes left. For example, a 15-minute chalkboard countdown would look like this

15   12   10   7   5   3   1

Cross off or erase the number of minutes left so that students can glance up at the board and make decisions to complete their work.

Elapsed Timer Displays

Many projected timers are available for sale through teacher material stores and online catalogues. Others are downloadable for use on your computer screen. Look for one that can display the elapsed time for an activity so that students can measure their progress against the time remaining to complete it.

Hit "Play"

Most students are familiar with the commands used to play digital movies and music (see Figure 19.1). Use your students' knowledge of the controls on digital devices to signal their use of time during activities and transitions. Review the commands on a remote control or other digital device:

- **Play.** Begin your work.
- **Pause.** Stop briefly to listen for further instructions.
- **Fast forward.** Increase the pace of your work.
- **Stop.** The time to work on this task has ended.
- **Rewind.** Go back to check the work you have completed.

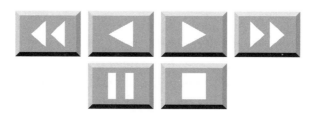

FIGURE 19.1. Hit "Play."

Musical Interludes

Students may require time to put away materials before moving on to the next activity. Play a recorded piece of music while students return supplies, hand in assignments, and replace furniture. These tasks should be completed by the time the song has finished. Good music selections include the theme song from the *Jeopardy* game show, Frederick Chopin's "Minute Waltz (which is closer to 2 minutes long), or any number of versions of "The Clean-Up Song." The use of a short piece of music is especially useful for younger children, who can use the audible cues to complete the transition.

Now You Try It

Identify the times in your daily schedule when a transition procedure is needed. Introduce your procedure during one transition and practice it each day until students are proficient. Expand the use of the procedure to other times throughout the day. When students are engaged in collaborative tasks that will take more than a few minutes, use a timer to signal the length of the activity. This will help you to keep the instructional pace you have established. It is especially useful for intermediate and secondary students to see the elapsed time displayed so that they gain experience at regulating the pace of their work, as well as making realistic estimates about the time needed for various tasks.

References

Good, T. L., & Brophy, J. E. (2003). *Looking in classrooms* (9th ed.). Boston: Pearson Allyn & Bacon.

Walberg, H. (1988). Synthesis of research on time and learning. *Educational Leadership, 45*(6), 76–85.

20

Distributing and Collecting Materials

GRADE LEVELS: K–12

Time Needed: 1 minute

What Is It?

Throughout the day teachers distribute and collect materials. Procedures for handling papers and equipment shorten transition times during the lesson and decrease the likelihood that misbehavior will occur. In addition, loss of student and classroom materials is reduced.

What Do I Do?

Distributing and Collecting Papers

Most teachers distribute papers by counting out the requisite number and handing the pile to the first person in the row. In turn, students take one and pass it to the person behind them. The process is reversed for collecting papers, beginning with the last student in the row. The problem is that this becomes an ideal time for students to talk because they have taken their eyes off of the teacher. To reduce the risk of misbehavior, distribute and collect papers *across* rows, as illustrated in Figure 20.1.

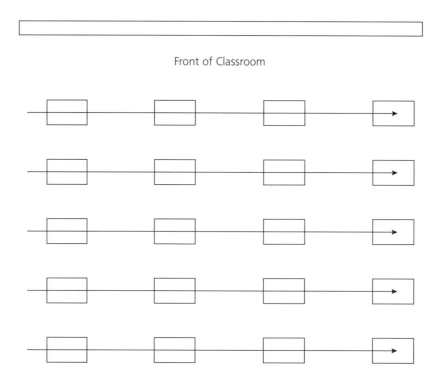

FIGURE 20.1. Map for distributing and collecting papers.

Magnetic Clips

This minimizes the number of times students must walk around the room to turn in papers. Attach a magnetic bulldog clip to the side of each desk. Students clip papers to be turned in throughout the day, then place them in the proper container when directed. In addition, it provides you with a quick visual gauge of an individual student's progress in completing his or her assignments. If you notice that a particular assignment is not yet on the magnetic clip, you can have a conversation with the student to find out what assistance he or she may need.

Numbering Classroom Equipment

Items like calculators, laptops, microscopes, dictionaries, and mathematics kits are costly (and sometimes impossible) to replace. For this reason, some teachers may be disinclined to give students easy access to them. However, this defeats the purpose of having these items in the first place. To prevent loss, number items with an indelible marker or label maker and place the same number on the shelf or storage container. Each student is given a number that corresponds with their place in your roll book. You will be able to identify missing items at a glance, as well as determine who was last using the item.

Valuable classroom equipment may be secured in a locked cabinet. For example, a laptop cart with chargers may be assigned to a particular classroom, grade level, or department. When using such items, make sure procedures are established for signing equipment in and out. This might consist of a sign-out sheet placed on a clipboard and attached to the cart. Some teachers collect student IDs to hold while the equipment is being used, and then return them when the item is replaced.

Collecting and Distributing Graded Work

Students submit a number of assignments each day. This quickly results in a blizzard of papers that need to be graded and returned. To keep papers organized, set up two plastic file crates and label them "Completed Work" and "Graded Work." Place a hanging file for each student labeled with his or her name and student number in the file crates. At the beginning of class students can place homework in one file and collect their graded work from the other. This system also allows you to monitor whether a particular student has turned in an assignment, or is failing to pick up graded work.

Now You Try It

Determine what procedures you will use to distribute and collect materials and add the necessary procedures to your classroom management plan. Make a list of organizational materials, including magnetic clips, file crates, and a labeling device, and check with your school's facilities manager for availability. While you may need to purchase some things with your own money, it is wise to find out what can be obtained for free at your school site.

21

Calling on Students

GRADE LEVELS: K–12

Time Needed: Less than 1 minute

What Is It?

Teachers call on students to respond to questions and participate in learning activities. However, the pattern of who is called upon is often uneven and may leave some students out of the conversation. For example, a study of questioning in elementary and middle school classrooms found that boys were called on more frequently than girls because they volunteered more often (Altermatt, Jovanovic, & Perry, 1998). You can use a system for drawing student names to ensure you are calling on everyone in your class.

An effective method for overcoming the limitations of calling on students disproportionately is to use a method for randomly calling on students. This allows several goals to be achieved simultaneously. The most obvious is that it decreases the likelihood that some students will be overlooked. Many secondary students have perfected the ability to remain unnoticed in classrooms, sitting quietly on the fringes of the classroom, and avoiding eye contact with the teacher. While the goal of a random questioning method is not to put students on the spot, it is to encourage other voices in the classroom discourse. In addition, it gives the teacher a richer and more nuanced portrait of the level of understanding the class possesses at a moment in time. If the only students who are called on are the ones who know the answer (and are therefore more likely to volunteer), then the teacher is not aware of what may need to be retaught, and to whom.

Do not use a random-question method as a way to catch students off guard. Always announce the student's name and make sure you have his or her attention before posing the question. This is respectful and contributes positively to the relationship between the teacher and the student. The idea is to reduce student passivity in the curriculum and increase participation. There is evidence that random questioning increases the level of student engagement and attention (Bonnstetter, 1988).

What Do I Do?

Craft Sticks

Write student names on wooden crafts sticks and place in a can. Draw names to respond.

Name Cards on a Ring

Write names on index cards and punch a hole in the top left corner. Place on a 2-inch binder ring and hang on a pushpin.

Playing Cards

Affix a playing card to each desk using tape and keep a matching deck for yourself. Draw cards to determine who will respond.

Seating Chart

Keep a seating chart inside a transparent sleeve. Use an erasable overhead pen to make tick marks on the chart to keep track of your questioning patterns.

Pass It On

After responding, allow the student to choose the next person. Be careful that this does not become a popularity contest.

Digital Name Generators

Many smartboards are equipped with a feature that can be programmed with the names of the students in your class. When activated, the student's name appears, often accompanied by a sound effect. You can then pose a question to him or her.

Now You Try It

It is important to remember that having a system for calling on students should never become a device for intimidating them. Avoid asking a question and then drawing a student name because it fosters a defensive atmosphere in the classroom. Instead, alert the student in advance before posing the question. When teaching this procedure to your students, make sure to include a "pass" policy any child may invoke when he or she does not want to answer. The request to pass a question to another must then be greeted with respect by the teacher.

References

Altermatt, E., Jovanovic, J., & Perry, M. (1998). Bias or responsivity? Sex and achievement-level effects on teachers' classroom questioning practices. *Journal of Educational Psychology, 90,* 516–527.

Bonnstetter, R. J. (1988). Active learning often starts with a question. *Journal of College Science Teaching, 18*(2), 95–97.

22

Organizing Materials

GRADE LEVELS: K–12

Time Needed: Several hours

What Is It?

Elementary and secondary classrooms are filled with books, equipment, writing instruments, paper . . . the list goes on and on. Easy access to these materials is essential for smooth instructional pacing. Effective teachers think carefully about how materials will be stored or displayed and then establish systems to organize items. This is especially true in small classrooms that have limited space for materials and children. When the teacher and students spend inordinate amounts of time searching for materials, instructional time is lost. In addition, the teacher who is constantly looking for materials projects a disorganized image to his or her students.

What Do I Do?

Student Work Displays

- Circular plastic laundry dryers have clips that can hold student work. Hang these around the classroom or over student desks for colorful and creative displays.
- Label 8.5″ × 11″ clear plastic pockets with the name of each student in your class and hang on a bulletin board. Have students review their work each week and select an item to place in their pocket.
- Hang items that need to be suspended from the ceiling with fishing line. It's strong, inexpensive, and almost invisible.

Book Display

- Plastic rain gutters are inexpensive and can be cut to any length. Purchase these from a home remodeling center and attach to the walls of your classroom. Use these gutters to display books from your classroom with covers showing to generate student interest and increase the likelihood they'll be chosen (Trelease, 2006). Bookstores display their books this way to generate sales.
- Label shelves and box baskets by genre to make it easy for selecting and replacing books.
- Bookmark frequently used Internet websites on the classroom computers so that students can readily find what they are looking for. The sites that receive the most use should be placed in the toolbar of the web browser.

Organizing and Storing Materials

- Hang language charts on a chart stand. Fold a sentence strip in half and cut a small hole in the center. Slide a hanger through the hole, then staple the top of the language chart inside the sentence strip. You can hang 200 language charts sideways on one chart stand (see Figure 22.1).

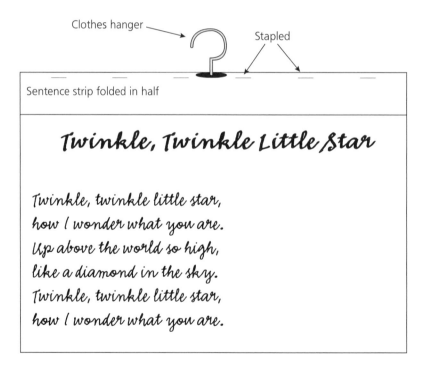

FIGURE 22.1. Mounting a language chart. From *Language Arts Workshop* (p. 51) by Nancy Frey and Douglas Fisher. Copyright 2003 by Prentice Hall, Inc. Reprinted by permission.

- Wrap posters and bulletin board displays in drycleaner bags before storing. Your materials will be in good shape when you use them again the following year.
- Very small items like paper clips, rubber bands, brads, and pushpins can be kept separated in lidded, sectioned plastic containers designed for fishing lures.
- Use snack-size Ziploc bags to organize letters for Making Words activities (Cunningham & Hall, 1994).
- Store unit materials by theme and clearly label boxes. Attach a list of what's in each box so you can locate items without taking apart your whole storage closet.

Ten Items to Keep in Your Classroom

1 **Fishing line.** For hanging things.

2 **Self-adhesive magnetic tape.** Cut with scissors and attach to the back of sentence strips to use on whiteboard.

3 **Self-adhesive Velcro strips.** Sticks anywhere.

4 **Ties.** Plastic twisty ties are great for securing wires and bundles of slim items.

5 **Trash bags.** For anything that needs a waterproof surface (they also make an excellent emergency raincoat!).

6 **Ziploc bags in assorted sizes.** Look for the ones that have a place to write on them.

7 **Magnets with clips.** Perfect for hanging things on the whiteboard or filing cabinet.

8 **Plastic and wooden clothespins.** Clip papers together.

9 **Plastic hangers.** Use to hang language charts and wet coats.

10 **Magnetic timer.** Keep it on your whiteboard and use it to monitor time for activities.

Now You Try It

Preparation is key in all aspects of teaching, and this applies to getting materials organized as well. These objects of everyday living can be found in discount and grocery stores, so stock up when they go on sale. Often, experienced teachers will purchase materials like these even before they know exactly what they are going to do with them. Families can also be a good source of items found around the home. Send a letter home to families asking them to save items you need for the classroom. When your materials are organized, you will discover that you can accomplish much more with your time.

References

Cunningham, P. M., & Hall, D. P. (1994). *Making words: Multilevel, hands-on, developmentally appropriate spelling and phonics activities*. Torrance, CA: Good Apple.

Trelease, J. (2006). *The read-aloud handbook* (6th ed.). New York: Penguin.

23

Assignment Headings

GRADE LEVELS: K–12

Time Needed: 5 minutes, repeated several times

What Is It?

Over the course of the school year, students will turn in a large number of assignments. Invariably, some of these papers will lack important information such as a name or date. Grading is further complicated when the topic of the assignment is unclear. It is useful to teach students a system for heading papers at the beginning of the year to make record keeping easier.

With the advent of digital resources, the naming of documents holds similar problems. It is difficult to process and locate 100 assignments that are all unhelpfully named "Term Paper." If your students are turning in digital assignments on a wiki, or through an e-platform, be sure to instruct them on properly naming the file so that you (and they) can locate it quickly. The title of the document should contain the student's last name, the name of the course, and a one- or two-word description.

What Do I Do?

You will need to determine the level of information necessary for your classroom. Certainly the student's first and last name and the date should be included on each paper. You may want them to also include the subject, period, and name of the assignment. Once you have settled on a format for headings, teach the procedure by modeling it daily through the first week of school. Consider posting an enlarged example and nonexample of the required heading, as shown in Figure 23.1.

Heading requirements	Example	Nonexample
First and last name	Melissa Smith	Melissa S.
Date	4-20-10 or April 20, 2010	April
Subject/Period	U.S. History/3	history
Assignment	p. 87, #1–5	questions

File-saving requirements	Example	Nonexample
Last name	Smith	Melissa
Subject/Period	U.S. History/3	history
Assignment	p. 87	questions
Extension	.doc	Left blank

FIGURE 23.1. Examples and nonexamples of required headings.

Now You Try It

Use headings as part of a mnemonic for students to recall how their papers should look. The HOW reminder serves as a simple rubric for grading the appearance of the paper (Archer & Gleason, 1994).

Heading.
Organized.
Written neatly.

Model each of these steps and provide examples and nonexamples so your students will understand your expectations. Follow up with individual students who do not consistently use properly formatted headings or file saving.

Reference

Archer, A., & Gleason, M. (1994). *Skills for school success*. North Billerica, MA: Curriculum Associates.

24

Teaching Students How to Request Help

GRADE LEVELS: K–12

Time Needed: 5-minute lessons taught daily for the first week

What Is It?

Students require assistance during their learning activities and are encouraged to seek help when needed. The ability to understand that help is needed represents a sophisticated metacognitive skill. As well, the student must possess a level of social and language skills to make the request. Learners who struggle with these social or language skills may forego asking for help because it is too difficult.

Student requests for help can also pose a management challenge for the teacher. If several students are asking at the same time, the teacher may have difficulty prioritizing. In these cases, it is often the more verbal and assertive students who receive the majority of the teacher's time. In addition, some students routinely stop working all together until they receive assistance. Establishing procedures for requesting help can provide support for students and organize the teacher's time.

What Do I Do?

Ask Three, Then Me

Even the youngest students can grasp the simplicity of this rule. Teach your students that when they need help with an academic task they should ask three classmates first before coming to you. This fosters cooperation and collaboration in your classroom.

The Batter's Box

In baseball, the player next up to bat waits quietly in the batter's box until it is his or her turn. In classrooms, students sometimes need to wait for their chance to talk with the teacher. Use colored tape to outline a $2' \times 2'$ box for a student to stand in when he or she needs help from the teacher. Place a box on the floor near the places you meet with students, including your desk and the guided-reading table.

Red Light, Green Light

Students needing help during independent work will stop working to raise their hand. Fearing that the teacher will not get to them, they keep their hand raised. It is preferable to establish a signal for help that allows the child to continue working until you get to him or her. Use a hot-glue gun to attach the lips of two small disposable bathroom cups, one red and one green, to each other and give one to each member of the class. When a student is working, the green cup should face up. When a student needs assistance, he or she turns it upside down so the red cup is on top. The teacher can easily scan the room to locate individuals who need assistance. Instruct them to continue working until you get to them. This is especially effective in the computer lab.

Call Button

Small battery-operated tap lights can be attached to the corner of students' desks using Velcro. When in need of help, the student taps on the light. One teacher likened this to the call button passengers use on airplanes to signal the flight attendant!

Now You Try It

Identify the times in your instructional day when a number of students are likely to need assistance. Establish a procedure for managing those high-demand times and include it in your classroom management plan.

25

Managing the Technology in Your Classroom

GRADE LEVELS: K–12

Time Needed: Not applicable

What Is It?

Technological displays have become ubiquitous in elementary and secondary classrooms. In particular, data projectors, document display cameras, and interactive whiteboards dominate most classrooms. In addition, teachers often use their own laptops to show students film clips and slide shows to support instruction. At one time, educational technology courses in teacher preparation programs featured extensive instruction on how to use technology. Today this is almost never addressed in any course, as educational technology courses have shifted attention to curricular and instructional matters.

What Do I Do?

Be Prepared!

- ◆ Don't waste instructional time starting up your display tools. Make sure these are on and working before class begins. Allow time to troubleshoot when simple fixes don't work.
- ◆ Keep an extra connector for your laptop and label it with your name. Put this in your desk drawer so that you have a spare when you need it.
- ◆ Rehearse using new technological tools before trying them in class. I have often seen new teachers struggling to make a complicated piece of equipment

work, turning their back to the class for minutes on end. This invites off-task and problem behaviors.

Tips for Effective Use of Data Projectors and Document Presenters

- Use pens in black or cool colors (blue, green, purple) for the majority of your writing. Save warm colors like yellow, orange, and red for underlining and highlighting key points.
- Turn off the display screen when students are speaking. It conveys your interest in what they are saying. Most of these technologies have a feature that allows you to darken the screen without shutting off the system.
- Place the display on your right if you are right-handed and left if you are left-handed. This allows you to operate it easily.
- Tape down the power cord so you don't trip on it.
- When making slides for a slide show, use a font size of at least 24. When displaying articles, worksheets, and other print material, enlarge the image for easier viewing.
- Use a laser pointer to focus student attention on a portion of the displayed information.
- Don't talk to the screen, talk to the students. They can't hear you when you turn your head.
- Don't forget to circulate throughout the classroom. It can become a habit to stay at the side of the display technology, especially interactive whiteboards. Proximity and circulation throughout the room are highly effective techniques for classroom management.

Instructional Uses

Document Center

Young students love using the document presenter. Invest in manipulatives such as letter tiles, numbers, and shapes. Let students complete activities using the document presenter.

Record Student Quotes

Circulate during small-group discussions and record student comments. Then display a summary of their comments on the document presenter. It is useful to attribute the ideas by name to review when the class comes back together as a large group. This increases accountability and motivation and fosters more productive conversations between students.

Encourage Student Use

These display technologies should not be confined to teacher use only. Make these technologies routinely available to students as they explain ideas and make formal presentations.

Now You Try It

Ask a colleague to observe you when you teach using display technologies. Get feedback about whether your use of the equipment contributes to or interferes with student learning.

26

Establishing and Maintaining a Course Website

GRADE LEVELS: K–12

Time Needed: Hours; ongoing

What Is It?

Students and families increasingly expect to be able to retrieve information at any-time of the day or week. Many districts routinely use e-platforms that all teachers are expected to use. In other cases, an individual teacher may set up a course website that contains helpful information for students and their families. Whether using a designed e-platform or an individual website several features should be in place to make it useful and easy to maintain.

What Do I Do?

Website design has advanced considerably since the early days of the World Wide Web. Most of us have been on websites that were distracting or unhelpful. This has, in part, led to the requirement by many schools and districts to include universal design principles that make website usage easier. This has been influenced in part by Section 508 of the Rehabilitation Act of 1998 that requires federal agencies and their affiliates to make websites accessible to people with disabilities. Many of these requirements are beneficial for all users. The Web Content Accessibility Guidelines 2.0 is available at *www.w3.org/TR/2008/REC-WCAG20-20081211*. They recommend that websites be

- **Perceivable.** Use color, background, and size of text judiciously to ensure that the information can be viewed.
- **Operable.** Make sure that the information can be driven by the keyboard and that anything timed for display (such as Flash animation) can be adjusted for speed.
- **Understandable.** Use developmentally appropriate text language and avoid placing too much text, or text that is too long, on a single page.
- **Robust.** The information should be useful and compatible with other technologies.

Designing Content for Your Classroom Website

The ultimate purpose of a classroom or course website is to make information readily available. In some cases, they are also used for interactive communication among students and with the teacher. Western Michigan University's education program makes several recommendations for structuring a website. Be sure to consult your school or district instructional technology coordinator for specific requirements about your course website.

Homepage

The homepage should contain the most frequently requested information, including your contact information (e-mail, mailing address of the school, room number), a description of the course, and a navigation bar for the other pages. While the homepage should be visually interesting, it should not be cluttered. Avoid using distracting backgrounds that make it difficult to read. Create a link to your school e-mail address so that students and families can readily contact you.

Student Page

This is the ideal place for your syllabus and classroom management plan, as well as a *current* list of assignments and projects. Nothing looks more dated than a website that features assignments that were due months ago. In some cases, you may also post handouts, but be sure to check the copyright before doing so. If your website is available to the general public, you will be restricted on what you can post. Consider featuring a reminder for students to contact you with questions, and update this information regularly so you can respond in a timely manner.

Family Page

The family page should contain information about grading, report cards, and setting up conferences. Provide helpful links for families seeking information, such as the school and district websites, content links, and information about your professional training and experiences.

Now You Try It

Consult with colleagues and the school's instructional technology coordinator to learn about the systems and requirements for establishing a course website. Take a look at other websites to get an idea of what you want for yours. Once you have designed the site, ask a student to navigate it to give you feedback about finding information. As always, update the information on your website regularly to ensure that it is useful.

Reference

W3C. (2008). Web content accessibility guidelines 2.0. Retrieved from *www.w3.org/TR/2008/REC-WCAG20-20081211*.

PART FOUR

Engaging Students through Peer Partners

27

Establishing Peer Partners

GRADE LEVELS: K–12

What Is It?

A central theory of the work of Russian psychologist Lev Vygotsky was that learners are supported through experiences within their zone of proximal development (ZPD) (Vygotsky, 1978). The ZPD is "the distance between the actual developmental level as determined by independent problem solving and the level of potential development as determined through problem solving under adult guidance, or in collaboration with more capable peers" (p. 86). In Vygotsky's words, the ZPD "awakens a variety of internal developmental processes that are able to operate only when the child is interacting with people in his environment" (p. 90). An important point, and one often missed in discussions of Vygotsky, focuses on the role that peers can play such that students work in their respective ZPDs. Given that there are significantly more peers than adults in most classroom environments, this is a resource that simply must be used if teachers are to be successful.

The benefits for peer partnerships extend to the more skilled student as well. Studies have shown that these include opportunities to review material and a deepening understanding of newly acquired skills and concepts (Moody, Vaughn, & Schumm, 1997; Tessier, 2007). Students working in peer partnerships are more likely to engage in academic risk taking, perhaps because neither is the expert (Kalkowski, 1995).

What Do I Do?

Students work in a variety of peer partnerships in the engaged classroom. Five specific roles are discussed in this section, but there are a few quality indicators that transcend each of these instructional arrangements.

1 **Partnerships are heterogeneous in nature.** Partner work is an ideal time to group students in mixed ability (heterogeneous) pairs. This grouping practice ensures that no partnerships are without a member skilled enough to successfully complete the task. A study of elementary students found that they prefer this arrangement for reading tasks (Elbaum, Schumm, & Vaughn, 1997).

2 **Partnerships are brief in nature.** Students should have experiences with a variety of classmates throughout the school year. Change partners frequently to foster a sense of community and expand the social and academic skills of your students. Chapter 33 features a list of ways to group students for partner work.

3 **Partnerships are not fixed.** Chapters 28–32 discuss five different partnership roles. However, no child should serve as all five kinds of partners to the same peer. After all, we're trying to create interdependence, not dependency.

4 **Students learn effective partnering skills through instruction.** Quality partnerships are not left to happenstance. Specific instruction of what occurs within the partnering activity is given before students work together. These instructions should be revisited throughout the school year.

5 **Assign numbers to partners for ease of instruction.** Number students as partner 1 or partner 2 so you can give directions quickly and efficiently. Determine which number will represent the more skilled students so you can assign them the modeling roles as needed.

6 **Monitor partnerships and intervene when there is difficulty.** Circulate and listen to the working conversations that happen in partners. Some dyads work better than others. If there is conflict between two students, be sure to intercede and help them resolve their difficulties.

Now You Try It

Read the following pages in this part for further explanation about the roles in peer partner work. Identify the opportunities within your curriculum for partner work and introduce the roles one at a time to ensure mastery.

References

Elbaum, B., Schumm, J., & Vaughn, S. (1997). Urban middle-elementary students' perceptions of grouping formats for reading instruction. *Elementary School Journal, 97,* 475–500.

Kalkowski, P. (1995). *Peer and cross-age tutoring: School improvement research series; Close-Up #18.* Portland, OR: Northwest Regional Educational Laboratory.

Moody, S. W., Vaughn, S., & Schumm, J. S. (1997). Instructional grouping for reading. *Remedial and Special Education, 18,* 347–356.

Tessier, J. (2007). Small-group peer teaching in an introductory biology classroom. *Journal of College Science Teaching, 36*(4), 64–69.

Vygotsky, L. S. (1978). *Mind and society: The development of higher mental processes.* Cambridge, MA: Harvard University Press.

Engaging Students through Peer Partners

28

Peer Partners Role 1
Response Partners

GRADE LEVELS: K–12

Time Needed: 15 minutes for initial instruction

What Is It?

Response partners are the most basic form of partnership in the interactive and engaged classroom. Students work in these partnerships to ask and answer questions, restate and recall information using tell–help–check, and brainstorm and refine ideas through think–pair–share. Because these partnerships are brief in duration, they are most easily organized by proximity.

What Do I Do?

Students need to be taught the skills necessary for effective conversation. Archer and Gleason (1994) advises that the following steps make expectations clear:

- **Look.** Make direct eye contact with your partner so you know you have his or her attention.
- **Lean.** Move your heads close together so you can be heard.
- **Whisper.** Partners speak to one another in a soft tone so as not to interfere with the learning of others. Reread "Monitoring Noise Level" in Part Three for ideas about teaching voice modulation.

Now You Try It

Examine your seating chart and identify the response pairs who will work with one another. Make adjustments to the classroom layout to facilitate ease of communication and lessen disruptions. For students who have not had an opportunity to interact with others as part of their school day, you might want to model this approach for the class and then invite students to the front of the room to demonstrate the approach in front of the class. After this "fishbowl" demonstration, be sure to highlight the components or features that you would like replicated by all students. You can also identify areas of potential concern and advise students about errors to avoid.

Reference

Archer, A., & Gleason, M. (1994). *Effective reading of textbooks*. Billerica, MA: Curriculum Associates.

29

Peer Partners Role 2
Reading Partners

GRADE LEVELS: K–12

Time Needed: 30 minutes for initial instruction

What Is It?

Students read a wide variety of materials during the course of the day. These reading materials may include textbooks, e-books, articles, newspapers, trade books, Internet pages, and directions. Reading partners support one another to boost comprehension and fill in knowledge gaps for one another across the genres and text types that students are expected to master.

What Do I Do?

Students read as partners for a variety of purposes. They can read to one another, read with one another, or review the content of a reading together.

Knee-to-Knee Reading

This exercise builds fluency and comprehension through repeated readings. Students turn to face one another so that their knees are touching. This distance allows them to hear one another without disturbing other reading pairs. Both students have a copy of the same text and select a passage for reading, placing their finger on the first word. The stronger reader goes first (remember that you have assigned numbers to the partners) while his or her partner follows along silently. Remind the silent readers to "read in your head" while listening to their partner. The roles are then reversed and the second reader rereads the passage. After reading the passage twice, partners retell the story and question one another about what they have just read.

Choral Reading

This exercise builds fluency, prosody (expression), and comprehension through repeated readings. Ideal selections for choral reading include poems, rhymes, and passages featuring dialogue. Students should *always* read the text silently first to increase comprehension. Cold reading of unfamiliar text interferes with comprehension, especially for struggling readers (Opitz & Rasinski, 2008). After reading the text, partners use a pencil or highlighter to mark phrase boundaries and pauses (Schreiber, 1991). After discussing the meaning of the passage, they read in unison several times in an effort to improve their performance and synchronize their reading.

ReQuest

This is a questioning technique for use with narrative and informational texts (Manzo, 1969). Reading partners read a text passage and question one another about the content. Roles are assigned and traded until the entire reading is completed. Task cards for completing ReQuest can be found in Form 29.1 at the end of this chapter.

Now You Try It

Identify the reading procedures that are most useful for your course content. Prepare language charts with the directions for each reading partner strategy you will use and display them in a prominent place in your classroom so students can reference them. As with other instructional routines, students should be taught the routines in advance of being expected to use them. For routines used while reading, it is helpful to have students practice the routine with texts at their independent reading levels and then use the routine with texts at students' instructional reading level.

References

Manzo, A. V. (1969). ReQuest procedure. *Journal of Reading, 13,* 123–126.

Opitz, M. F., & Rasinski, T. V. (2008). *Good-bye round robin: 25 effective oral reading strategies* (2nd ed.). Portsmouth, NH: Heinemann.

Schreiber, P. S. (1991). Understanding prosody's role in reading acquisition. *Theory Into Practice, 30,* 158–164.

ReQuest Role Cards

ReQuest questioner

1   Read the text passage silently and look for important details.

2   After reading, write several questions about the passage.

3   Keep your book open and ask your partner the questions. Listen to his or her answers and check the reading to make sure it is correct.

4   If his or her answer is not correct, ask another question or give a hint to help him or her answer the question. Show your partner the answer in the text.

5   When you're finished, trade roles for the next passage.

ReQuest respondent

1   Read the text passage silently and look for important details.

2   After reading, write several questions you think your partner will ask you about the passage.

3   Close your book and listen carefully to the questions. Recall the information in the reading and answer the questions. You can ask your partner to clarify the meaning of the question if you do not understand.

4   Your partner will show you the answers in the text to any questions you cannot answer.

5   When you're finished, trade roles for the next passage.

••••••••••••••••• **30** •••••••••••••••••

Peer Partners Role 3
On-Task Partners

GRADE LEVELS: K–12

Time Needed: 5 minutes for initial instruction

What Is It?

Every learner has occasional lapses in attention and can quickly fall behind the classroom instruction. We've all had this experience and know exactly what it feels like. Successful students know how to get themselves back on track. On-task partners monitor each other to ensure both are accurately following the teacher's directions thus building habits to refocus and reengage when attention lapses.

What Do I Do?

Instruct students that one of the responsibilities they have within their classroom community is to watch out for one another. An important way this can be accomplished is by helping each other when someone loses his or her place or is having difficulty with following a direction given by the teacher.

When a direction is given to read or do something, on-task partners should follow these steps:

1 Follow the direction given by the teacher.

2 Check to see whether your partner is doing the same thing.

3 If your partner is not, quietly help him or her.

Students should also be taught how help can be offered. This can begin with a brainstorming of ideas for helping one another.

- Point to a place on his or her paper or in his or her book with your finger or pencil.
- Open his or her book to the correct page.
- Show him or her the page you are on.
- Place your hand softly on his or her shoulder to get his or her attention.
- Help him or her locate an item he or she is missing.

Now You Try It

Offering help is an important social skill all students need to master. Ask your students how they help one another in class—you may be surprised at the many ideas they offer! Be sure to also address how help is accepted and acknowledged, including smiling, making eye contact, and nodding.

31

Peer Partners Role 4
Assignment Partners

GRADE LEVELS: K–12

Time Needed: 5–10 minutes

What Is It?

Assignment partners are responsible for consulting with each other about home-work and in-class assignments. Following an absence, the partners meet to review the collected assignment information and handouts from the attendance monitor (see Chapter 15 for a discussion about what to do when a student is absent).

What Do I Do?

Designate assignment partners at the beginning of each term to make sure that every student has at least one classmate to consult. Students may or may not decide to exchange contact information; no one should feel pressured into doing so. If you use assignment partners, build a few minutes into your schedule several times a week for students to discuss the contact details and ask clarifying questions.

Now You Try It

Develop a list of assignment partners in your classroom. Remember that these do not need to be classmates who are in close proximity but should be students who can interact positively with one another. You might want to post this list in a public place to increase accountability and to provide students with a visual reminder that one of their roles is monitoring assignments that are missed by their partner. Because of the ongoing nature of the assignment partner role, it is advisable to change these less frequently.

32

Peer Partners Role 5
Collaborative Partners

GRADE LEVELS: K–12

Time Needed: Multiple lessons

What Is It?

The most complex partnering arrangement is the collaborative one. Students in collaborative partnerships work together for a longer period of time on an assignment or project for which they are jointly accountable. Collaborative partners may be teamed with another dyad to form a group of four. The effectiveness of cooperative learning has been studied for decades and found to have a positive effect on achievement, social skills, and motivation (Johnson & Johnson, 1999; Slavin, 1995). Although a majority of teachers report using cooperative learning in their classrooms, they also report difficulties with managing the movement of students and in structuring tasks that allow all students to participate equitably (Tomlinson, Moon, & Callahan, 1998). To be effective, these groups need a meaningful task, individual and group accountability, and opportunities to interact (Frey, Fisher, & Everlove, 2009).

What Do I Do?

Use collaborative learning arrangements regularly to make it easier to establish more formal productive learning groups later. These collaborative partnerships form the heart of a cooperative learning group because working relationships have been fostered in the dyads or triads. Because cooperative learning groups are so useful in academically diverse classrooms, it is advisable to look to these quality indicators in collaborative partnerships as well (Johnson & Johnson, 1999).

1 **Positive interdependence.** Materials, resources, information, and tasks are shared by the partners, who are also jointly accountable for the end product.

2 **Face-to-face interaction.** The task should be completed in the presence of one another. For example, a report on the causes and effects of World War II should not be divided and written at home.

3 **Individual accountability.** Partners receive an individual grade as well as a project grade. Partners self-assess their performance and give feedback about the assignment. A sample appears in Form 32.1 at the end of this chapter.

4 **Instruction in social interactions.** Rules and procedures are in place to facilitate efficient work between partners. In addition, the teacher offers intentional instruction on questioning, problem solving, and communication.

5 **Group processing.** Partners have an opportunity to discuss how their work is progressing and address difficulties with one another.

Now You Try It

Design a fun task to use as an introduction to collaborative partners. The first tasks should be easier to accomplish so that students can concentrate on the intricacies of working together in a collaborative way. As you introduce increasingly complex tasks, students should be reminded to rely on their group members and to individually produce their respective parts.

References

Frey, N., Fisher, D., & Everlove, S. (2009). *Productive group work: How to engage students, build teamwork, and promote understanding.* Alexandria, VA: Association for Supervision and Curriculum Development.

Johnson, D. W., & Johnson, R. T. (1999). *Learning together and alone: Cooperative, competitive, and individualistic learning* (5th ed.). Boston: Allyn & Bacon.

Slavin, R. E. (1995). *Cooperative learning: Theory, research, and practice* (2nd ed.). Boston: Allyn & Bacon.

Tomlinson, C. A., Moon, T. R., & Callahan, C. M. (1998). How well are we addressing academic diversity in the middle school? *Middle School Journal, 29*(3), 3–11.

Self-Assessment for Collaborative Partner Work

Name: _____ Date: _____

Assignment: _____

_____

_____

_____

Rank yourself on how well you accomplished these goals.

1 = always

2 = almost always

3 = sometimes

4 = hardly ever

5 = never

I shared materials and information with my partner.	**1**	**2**	**3**	**4**	**5**
I listened respectfully to my partner and used some of his or her ideas.	**1**	**2**	**3**	**4**	**5**
I shared my ideas with my partner.	**1**	**2**	**3**	**4**	**5**
My work on this project represents my best efforts.	**1**	**2**	**3**	**4**	**5**
I completed my tasks on time.	**1**	**2**	**3**	**4**	**5**

The best thing about this assignment was _____.

_____

_____

Here are the things you should change next time _____

_____

_____

33

Grouping Students Efficiently

GRADE LEVELS: K–12

Time Needed: 1–3 minutes

What Is It?

Much of the work done in engaging classrooms is accomplished through peer partnerships. These partnerships build a sense of community in the classroom because students learn how to give and receive help. While these partnerships form the basis for much of the instruction in the classroom, there are other times when you need to form temporary groups to complete an activity. These groups may be random in nature but they should not be haphazard. Announcing that everyone should "find a group" can lead to lost instructional time and marginalization for some students who are left out.

What Do I Do?

There are a number of ways to group students. These differ based on the tasks students are expected to complete. For example, random groups are effective ways to build social skills and to ensure that students learn to interact with a wide range of people. Random groups are also good for learning tasks that are relatively brief in nature. Student-choice groups are useful when students are completing tasks based on their interests. Student-choice groups are also effective when students complete part of the tasks outside of the classroom. Finally, teacher-choice groups are effective when the tasks require diverse perspectives and when students are expected to produce individually as part of the learning environment.

Random Groupings

◆ **Playing cards.** Distribute cards and group students by matching numbers or suits.

◆ **Famous pairs.** Find a partner by matching index cards with the names of famous pairs:

> Lucy and Ethel
> Peanut butter and jelly
> Alexander Hamilton and Aaron Burr
> Math equation and correct answer

◆ *Puzzles.* Create a four-piece puzzle that forms a shape. Students complete the puzzle and form a group.

◆ *Count off.* Students count off from one to five to determine a group assignment. Tell young students to place the corresponding number of fingers into the palm of their hand to remember their assignment.

◆ *Busy bees.* This is a rapid regrouping strategy for primary grades. When students have a series of tasks to do with several partners, have them move like busy bees. On your cue, children make a buzzing sound and move slowly around the classroom until you tell them to "land." They turn to the person next to them to complete the task, then "fly" again to find a new partner.

◆ *Colors and shapes.* Very young children can locate group members by using shapes cut from construction paper.

◆ *Bus stop.* Sometimes students have difficulty locating their group. Hang a sign that says "Bus Stop" in an area of the classroom for students to stand near when they cannot find members of their group. Classmates should walk by the bus stop whenever they see someone waiting there.

Student-Choice Groups

As the name implies, there are times in which students select their own group members. As their teacher, you simply need to set the parameters, including how many people can be in a group (e.g., groups must be between four and six students) and how they select group members. Some teachers ask students to write down several names for potential group members and then form the groups based on these requests. Others invite students to talk with one another and propose groups. Again, these groups are time limited and focused on a specific task, usually a task based on interests and out-of-class work.

Teacher-Choice Groups

Students can be grouped by the teacher according to a variety of characteristics, including:

- ◆ **Interest.** Students select their group by topic.
- ◆ **Learning styles.** Auditory, visual, and kinesthetic.
- ◆ **Temperament.** Assign roles to provide multiple experiences with leadership roles.
- ◆ **Ability.** Reading or math levels.
- ◆ **Expertise.** Experience with a particular topic.

One common way for teachers to group students for collaborative tasks or productive group work is by ranking the class on skill level, from the top-performing student to the lowest-performing student. Privately, the teacher then cuts the list at the midpoint and forms groups by selecting students from each list. For example, for their collaborative learning groups in math, the teacher listed the 30 students in order of skill based on the most recent formative assessment. The list was cut in half after student 15. Then students 1, 2, 16, and 17 were grouped together. Students 3, 4, 18, and 19 were grouped together, and so on. In this way, every group contains diverse membership but not so diverse that the group cannot produce.

Another teacher-choice group is constructed for instruction based on need. For example, while the rest of the class works on their collaborative tasks, the teacher may meet with four students who have similar instructional needs. The teacher has chosen these students based on assessment information and will provide instruction and intervention to build the students' skills.

Now You Try It

Consider the tasks you want students to complete and match those to grouping strategies. When you have selected the appropriate grouping strategy, form the groups. Be careful not to miss social cues about students who might require minor changes in groups, such as two students with histories of fighting who might be better off in different groups. Make your expectations for group work clear as you form the groups so that students know how to work and what to produce.

PART FIVE

Engaging Students for Learning

34

Interest Surveys

GRADE LEVELS: K–12

Time Needed: 15 minutes to administer; longer to analyze; even longer to integrate topics into discussions and readings

What Is It?

The relationship between teacher and student begins on the first day of school as both get to know one another. Important sources of information about the student include the cumulative files, school records, and reports from previous teachers. Sometimes overlooked is the source itself—the student. Interest surveys can yield valuable information to be utilized in your planning for instruction. These surveys are usually in written form, although they can be administered orally as well using an interview format.

What Do I Do?

The most successful interest surveys use language that is developmentally appropriate for students. For younger students, these may include graphics for easy response. Older students can complete open-response questions that allow them to answer in their own words. Many teachers construct their own surveys to tailor them to the classroom and broader community. Sample elementary and secondary interest surveys are included here for you to use or modify (see Forms 34.1 and 34.2, respectively, at the end of this chapter).

Before administering a survey, discuss the purpose with your students. In particular, emphasize that this is not a test and is given so you can be a better teacher for each of them. You may want to share a survey you have completed after students are finished so they can become better acquainted with you. (Sharing yours before students have completed the survey can influence their answers.)

Now You Try It

After administering the surveys, construct a chart to note results. Look for items students have in common with one another. These insights can serve as a good first step in fostering positive peer relationships in the classroom. These insights can also be used to recommend readings and to make connections to course content. For example, a student who is interested in the night sky might be a useful resource for other students during units of study related to astronomy. A student who enjoys poetry might want to share a related poem with the class.

Interest Survey for Younger Students

All about Me

My name is _____

I circled all the things I am very good at doing:

helping people	*running*	*tying shoes*
being a friend	*jumping*	*reading*
telling jokes	*climbing*	*writing*
sharing	*helping animals*	*math*

I circled all the things I need help doing:

helping people	*running*	*tying shoes*
being a friend	*jumping*	*reading*
telling jokes	*climbing*	*writing*
sharing	*helping animals*	*math*

My three favorite things to read and talk about are:

1. _____

2. _____

3. _____

Here is a picture of me doing something that makes me happy.

Interest Survey for Older Students.

Name: _____ **Date:** _____

Subject/Period: _____

Directions: Please complete each statement in your own words.

1 The subject I enjoy most in school is _____ because
_____

2 The subject I like least in school is _____ because
_____

3 I am happiest when _____

4 The time of day I enjoy most is _____

5 The three words that best describe me are _____ and
_____ and _____

6 People ask me for help with _____

7 I sometimes need help with _____

8 I hope this class is _____ because
_____

9 I hope we will get a chance to talk and read about these topics: _____
_____
_____

10 Here are some things you need to know about me:
_____
_____
_____
_____
_____
_____
_____
_____

35

Bellwork

GRADE LEVELS: K–12

Time Needed: 5–10 minutes

What Is It?

Bellwork is a form of writing to learn that invites students to consider the topic of your class for the day. You may recall from the discussion in Chapter 14 on taking attendance that it is also a procedure that gets students working as soon as they enter the classroom. A writing prompt is posted on the whiteboard before class begins. Students follow the procedures you have established for entering the classroom and then begin writing. The response continues until the bell has rung several minutes later.

Writing to learn is an instructional strategy that invites students to recall what they know, ask questions about what they do not yet know, or respond to a thought-provoking question (Sorcinelli & Elbow, 1997). This type of writing is described as "low-stakes writing" because is not evaluated in the same way as a finished piece. Writing to learn differs from process writing precisely because students do not go through the many steps of drafting, revision, and editing associated with process writing.

Bellwork can assume a variety of forms, including Yesterday's News, Crystal Ball, awards, Headline News, cinquains, Take a Stand, and Exit Slips (Fisher & Frey, 2008).

What Do I Do?

Yesterday's News

This prompt signals students to compose a summary of what was learned in the previous class. Students who were absent can read the summary by their assignment partner to review missing material.

Crystal Ball

Students write a prediction of what might be discussed in today's class, based on the topic from the previous day.

Awards

Learners write a nomination and rationale for an award of the teacher's creation related to the topic of study. For example, a science teacher might ask for a nomination for the most influential discovery of the 20th century.

Headline News

This activity is great for social studies classes. Have students write headlines for newspapers from around the world on an event being studied in class. For instance, students in world history can compose headlines on the bombing of Pearl Harbor for American, Japanese, and German newspapers.

Cinquains

A five-line poem related to a content topic is written using a formula. The first line consists of a noun, while the second line describes the noun in two words. Three words ending in *ing* comprise the third line, and the fourth line is a four-word description of the topic. The last line is a synonym for the noun in the first line. A fifth-grade student wrote the following cinquain on the bravery of Rosa Parks:

Patriot
Rosa Parks
Waiting, refusing, protesting
Arrested by Birmingham police
Hero

Take a Stand

Post a statement on the board and have students write for 5 minutes on evidence in support of the statement, then an additional 5 minutes on evidence challenging the statement. For example, a seventh-grade teacher posts the statement "School uniforms have a positive effect on middle school campuses" to introduce persuasive essays.

Exit Slips

Although not a traditional bellwork activity because it does not come at the start of class, exit slips are a useful way to have students summarize a lesson. Exit slips are composed during the last 5 minutes of class and handed to the teacher when students are dismissed.

Now You Try It

Create a plan for introducing bellwork into your classroom routine. During the first week these writing events should occur after class has started so you can model what is expected. If you get stuck on prompts, take a look at the many websites featuring writing prompts. A particularly imaginative one can be found at *www.creativity-portal.com/prompts/imagination.prompt.html* that contains ideas like "What would happen if you didn't leave the house this morning?"

References

Creativity Portal. (n.d.). 365 picture prompts. Retrieved from *www.creativity-portal.com/prompts/imagination.prompt.html*.

Fisher, D., & Frey, N. (2008). *Improving adolescent literacy: Content area reading strategies at work* (2nd ed.). Upper Saddle River, NJ: Merrill Prentice-Hall.

Sorcinelli, M. D., & Elbow, P. (Eds). (1997). *Writing to learn: Strategies for assigning and responding to writing across the disciplines*. San Francisco: Jossey-Bass.

36

RAFT
(Role–Audience–Format–Topic)

GRADE LEVELS: 2–12

Time Needed: 10–30 minutes

What Is It?

RAFT is a writing frame that emphasizes perspective and literary response (Santa & Havens, 1995). It is flexible because the frame lends itself to writing across the curriculum.

> **RAFT stands for:**
>
> **R**ole of the writer [Who is the writer?]
> **A**udience [Who is the reader?]
> **F**ormat [What format will be used?]
> **T**opic [What is the subject of the piece?]

Students use the RAFT writing frame to create a piece that exhibits voice, purpose, structure, and focus. The teacher creates a RAFT that invites students to integrate what they know about a topic using a creative and engaging approach. For instance, a third-grade science teacher had students write a RAFT that encouraged them to use what they had learned about pollination.

R—Flower
A—Honey bee
F—Invitation
T—Please come to visit

What Do I Do?

Once students become comfortable with using the RAFT writing frame, you can extend its use. Assign half the class a RAFT taking the perspective of one historical figure while the other students write a competing RAFT with an alternative perspective.

R—General Santa Anna	**R**—Texas patriots
A—rebels hiding in the Alamo	**A**—Santa Anna
F—declaration of war	**F**—letter of response
T—surrender now or face attack	**T**—Texas declares independence from Mexico

Note the differences in how the audience is perceived depending on the role of the writer. After students write their RAFTs, move to collaborative partners and have them share their letters with one another.

Reference

Santa, C., & Havens, L. (1995). *Creating independence through student-owned strategies: Project CRISS*. Dubuque, IA: Kendall-Hunt.

37

Community Surveys

GRADE LEVELS: K–12

Time Needed: Span of several days to collect and analyze data

What Is It?

Community surveys allow students to interview participants about a topic of study. These surveys also provide an opportunity for students to connect their schoolwork with perspectives from the larger community. A community can be defined as narrowly as the classroom or grade level, or as broadly as the school or outside community. This activity combines subject-area learning with mathematics instruction as students identify and categorize responses. The analysis of the survey data should be developmentally appropriate for the students. Primary students will count results, while intermediate students can compute fractions. Survey data is an excellent tool for teaching statistical techniques to secondary students.

What Do I Do?

For young students, begin with a survey of the class on a topic like the number of siblings or types of pets and graph the results. Design a question of interest with your class and discuss whom they will survey. Questions may be general in nature:

- ◆ "What is your favorite cafeteria lunch?"
- ◆ "Who do you depend on?"
- ◆ "What is the best book you ever read?"

Questions may also be more specific and related directly to the content you are teaching. An eighth-grade algebra teacher had students survey volunteers at the school by asking them to correctly solve an equation. (It should be noted that this was done with permission from the principal and support from the faculty at the school.) The results of the survey spurred a lively debate in the class about mathematical knowledge! The students in the class then visited the volunteer participants and taught a short lesson on solving the equation. The lessons were videotaped and discussed in the algebra class and results of the pre- and posttest surveys were computed.

Now You Try It

Develop a survey question for students to conduct in the classroom and teach the necessary tabulation skills needed to analyze the data. In addition to gaining an understanding of data collection and analysis, students will know more about themselves and the people around them.

38

Human Graphs

GRADE LEVELS: K–12

Time Needed: 15–20 minutes

What Is It?

Students begin to learn to represent data using graphing techniques from the time they begin school. However, graphing is often taught only within the confines of mathematics instruction. Human graphs are a means for using graphs across the curriculum to engage students in a variety of ways to represent information. Students line up and use their bodies to represent data.

What Do I Do?

Students can move into a variety of configurations to illustrate graphing techniques. Take photographs of students posing as graphs so they can see how the information was represented.

Histogram

Students line up shoulder-to-shoulder from shortest to tallest. This helps them to remember that the columns of a histogram are continuous.

Bar Graph

Distribute sandwich cookies to the class and ask them to eat the cookie, then write down how they ate it (twisted top off and ate cream first, ate cookie in one bite, twisted top off and ate lid first, etc.). Tape category labels to the wall and have students line up single file in front of the correct label. The resulting student lines illustrate a bar graph.

Stem-and-Leaf Graph

A stem-and-leaf graph organizes data to show both shape and distribution. You will need to prepare number cards in advance of this activity. Have students line up according to the day of the month their birthday occurs. For instance, a student with a birthday of October 25 stands with the people whose birthday occurs between the 20th and 29th of the month. All the "twenties" further arrange their line from zero to nine. Students hold number cards as place markers for each digit.

Cartesian Coordinates

Go outdoors to illustrate x–y coordinates on a graph marked with colored chalk on the cement. Students hold cards representing arbitrary coordinates and locate themselves on the graph. This graphing technique is an excellent method for representing positions on a map.

Value Lines

This graphing technique is useful for representing the gamut of opinions about a particular subject (Kagan, 1990). Pose a thought-provoking question related to your content and ask students to place themselves on a line representing a continuum of responses. For example, students in an AP American literature class considered the question, "Should our school district ban certain books from high school classrooms?" The teacher placed posters that read "I strongly agree" and "I strongly disagree" on opposite walls and asked students to locate themselves on the line. She then found the center of the line and had half the line take two steps out and walk to the end of the original line. This resulted in students who located themselves near the middle of the continuum speaking to someone near an extreme of the continuum (Kagan, 1990).

Now You Try It

Examine your curriculum content for information that is represented through graphs. Having students create these graphs helps them understand the content in new and different ways. The human graph strategy works well in conjunction with community surveys.

Reference

Kagan. S. (1990). *Cooperative learning*. San Clemente, CA: Kagan.

39

Establishing Purpose

GRADE LEVELS: K–12

Time Needed: About 10 minutes per day

What Is It?

The process of establishing purpose involves making sure that students understand what they will be learning and what they will be doing with this new learning (Fisher, Frey, & Rothenberg, 2008). It is not uncommon for teachers to list purposes (sometimes called objectives) in lesson plans, but these are rarely shared with students. However, establishing purpose is a particularly robust practice for ELLs (Hill & Flynn, 2006). The purpose of a lesson is different from the standard from which it is derived. Content standards are typically broad and require many lessons and experiences before reaching mastery. The purpose, on the other hand, is specific to the lesson being taught. It is also not a statement of an activity, such as "take a test." The purposes involve the content, language, and social goals of the lesson.

What Do I Do?

When designing your lesson, consider the content purpose of the lesson. While the purpose stems from a standard, they are not the standard itself. For example, a content purpose for a specific lesson might be "understand the events that led up to the assassination of Archduke Franz Ferdinand," which is a portion of the standard that reads, "Explain the causes of World War I." Once the content purpose is clear, consider what the language demands for the lesson will be. Language purposes are the reading, writing, speaking, listening, and viewing that will be necessary. For instance, the lesson's language purpose might be "to construct a timeline of the events leading up to and immediately after the assassination." Finally, the social purpose concerns students' interactions that occur during the lesson, especially with their peers. Therefore, the social purpose for the lesson would be "to work collaboratively with your group to develop a timeline poster."

Now You Try It

Some teachers post the purposes on the whiteboard at the beginning of a lesson. While this is not a requirement, it can be quite helpful for focusing student attention and keeping you on track during your lesson. Post the purposes and review them at the beginning of the lesson, and return to them at the end to provide reinforcement of learning and closure to the lesson.

References

Fisher, D., Frey, N., & Rothenberg, C. (2008). *Content-area conversations: How to plan discussion-based lessons for diverse language learners*. Alexandria, VA: Association for Supervision and Curriculum Development.

Hill, J. D., & Flynn, K. M. (2006). *Classroom instruction that works with English language learners*. Alexandria, VA: Association for Supervision and Curriculum Development.

40

Vocabulary Routines

GRADE LEVELS: K–12

Time Needed: About 10 minutes per day

What Is It?

Vocabulary is a significant predictor of understanding. When the listener or reader knows the words that the speaker or writer is using, comprehension is better. Not understanding the words compromises understanding and interferes with meaning making. Of course there is a great deal of evidence suggesting that teachers should focus on vocabulary learning daily (Beck, McKeown, & Kucan, 2002; Bromley, 2007).

What Do I Do?

While there are a vast number of ways to engage students in vocabulary learning, there are specific ways that are high utility and fairly easy to implement. When the following four routines are integrated into the classroom, I suggest you engage in additional reading about effective vocabulary instruction to validate and expand your repertoire (e.g., Frey & Fisher, 2009; Nagy, 1988).

  ◆ **Word walls.** Teachers post 5 to 10 words on a wall space that is easily visible from anywhere in the room. The purpose of the word wall is to remind teachers to look for ways to bring words they want students to own back into the conversation so that students get many and varied experiences with the words (Ganske, 2006, 2008).

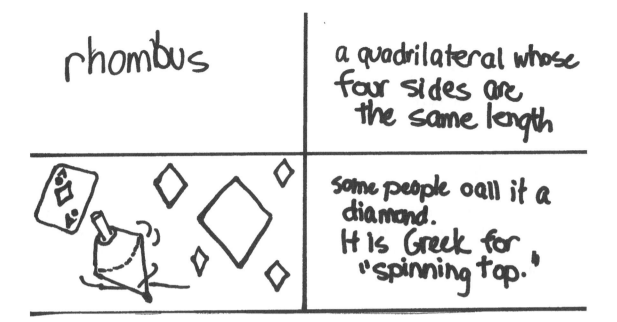

FIGURE 40.1. Sample word card.

- **Word cards.** Students analyze a word for its meaning, what it doesn't mean, and create a visual reminder. A sample card for the word *rhombus* can be seen in Figure 40.1.
- **Word sorts.** Students arrange a list of words by their features. Word sorts can be open (students are not provided with categories) or closed (students are provided categories in which to sort). An example of a word sort in which words could be used more than once can be found in Figure 40.2.
- **Word games.** Students play with words and their meanings. For example, this might involve a Bingo game of sorts (Cunningham & Hall, 1994) where

Homonym	Homophone	Homograph
charge	bear/bare	bass
goal	board/bored	lead
plant	find/fined	live
spring	pray/prey	read

FIGURE 40.2. Sample word sort.

students write words from the class in various squares and then the teacher randomly draws definitions until someone gets bingo. We also like games such as *Jeopardy, Who Wants to Be a Millionaire?*, or *$25,000 Pyramid*, as they allow students to review words while having a bit of fun. A great website that provides information about vocabulary games is *jc-schools.net/tutorials/vocab/ppt-vocab.html* (Fisher, Frey, & Anderson, 2010, p. 153).

Now You Try It

After modeling the use of each of these vocabulary routines with the class, integrate these routines into the class structure. You don't need to use all of them every day, but rather use at least one of them per day. In this way, your students will be well on their way to word learning and better understanding.

References

Academic vocabulary. (n.d.). PowerPoint games. Retrieved from *jc-schools.net/tutorials/vocab/ppt-vocab.html*.

Beck, I. L., McKeown, M. G., & Kucan, L. (2002). *Bringing words to life: Robust vocabulary instruction*. New York: Guilford Press.

Bromley, K. (2007). Nine things every teacher should know about words and vocabulary instruction. *Journal of Adolescent and Adult Literacy, 50*, 528–537.

Cunningham, P. E., & Hall, D. P. (1994). *Making words: Multilevel hands-on, developmentally appropriate spelling and phonics activities*. Torrance, CA: Good Apple.

Fisher, D., Frey, N., & Anderson, H. (2010). Thinking and comprehending in the mathematics classroom (pp. 146–159). In K. Ganske & D. Fisher (Eds.), *Comprehension across the curriculum: Perspectives and practices, K–12*. New York: Guilford Press.

Frey, N., & Fisher, D. (2009). *Learning words inside and out: Vocabulary instruction that boosts achievement in all subject areas*. Portsmouth, NH: Heinemann.

Ganske, K. (2006). *Word sorts and more: Sound, pattern and meaning explorations K–3*. New York: Guilford Press.

Ganske, K. (2008). *Mindful of words: Spelling and vocabulary explorations 4–8*. New York: Guilford Press.

Nagy, W. E. (1988). *Teaching vocabulary to improve reading comprehension*. Newark DE: International Reading Association.

41

Whip-Around

GRADE LEVELS: K–12

Time Needed: 5 minutes

What Is It?

A whip-around (Harmin, 1994) is a method for reporting ideas developed during small-group brainstorming sessions. Students are instructed to write their thoughts on a list for sharing with the class. Every student stands and the first group presents their first idea. The other groups consult their list to see whether they have a similar response. If so, they place a check mark next to the item. The second group then shares one idea and all groups check off any similar ideas. Each group reports one idea until original responses have been stated. When a group has no more responses to offer, the members sit down. A whip-around eliminates repetition and fosters listening skills because everyone must attend to the responses of others. A whip-around can be done in small student-led groups as well.

What Do I Do?

Teachers sometimes forgo brainstorming or group reports because they are time-consuming. A whip-around tightens the presentations by emphasizing original ideas. It also serves as confirmation of students' thinking because they hear others stating similar responses.

Now You Try It

Assist students who are still learning whip-around by prompting them to check their lists after each idea. You can follow up a whip-around by tallying the number of times a response was recorded by a group.

Reference

Harmin, M. (1994). *Inspiring active learning: A handbook for teachers.* Alexandria, VA: Association for Supervision and Curriculum Development.

42

Response Cards

GRADE LEVELS: K–12

Time Needed: 5–15 minutes

What Is It?

Response cards are used by students to answer questions posed by the teacher. They are held up to indicate their answer, providing the teacher with a quick assessment. Response cards increase student participation and learning because everyone can answer (Kellum, Carr, & Dozier, 2001). Response cards can be prepared in advance for predictable answers, or made of a material that allows the student to write an original answer.

What Do I Do?

Prepared Cards

Cards can be prepared for student use and distributed in advance. Prepared cards are an excellent tool for reviewing facts, although they assess recognition only. Prepared cards can be constructed for any topic, and dichotomous cards (two choices) can be written on both sides to save paper. Consider using cards of different colors to make it easier for you to gauge responses.

- True–false
- Yes–no
- Truth–myth
- Vocabulary terms
- Mathematics symbols

Constructed Response Cards

These allow students to construct original answers and hold them up for the teacher to review. Math problems, spelling words, and diagrams can all be scribed on the board. The pacing is somewhat slower because students need more time to write their answers. Examples of boards include:

- ◆ Write-on boards
- ◆ Chalkboards
- ◆ Transparent report covers with a white cardboard inset to create a firm writing surface

A relatively inexpensive alternative is to visit a home-improvement center for showerboard, thin sheets of wood covered with laminate. These are sold in 4′ × 8′ sheets and can be cut to any size. The surface on these will not last as long as the commercially prepared write-on boards, but are considerably less expensive.

Now You Try It

Give students many opportunities to use their response cards by posing questions frequently. This increases engagement while providing opportunities for repetition and rehearsal. If using prepared response cards, begin with only a small number and increase choices over time. Response cards can also be shared by response partners, thereby saving on the number of materials.

References

Kellum, K. K., Carr, J. E., & Dozier, C. L. (2001). Response-card instruction and student learning in a college classroom. *Teaching of Psychology, 28*, 101–104.

43

Walking Review

GRADE LEVELS: K–12

Time Needed: 10–15 minutes

What Is It?

A walking review is an interactive instructional method for providing students with an opportunity to work collaboratively with peers to review previously taught material. Because this process involves student discussion and writing, learners can explain solutions to their peers, ask clarifying questions, consult outside references, and practice writing correct answers. In addition, the classroom community is strengthened by the necessary interaction with classmates that is required in order to successfully complete the activity. Finally, students learn to appreciate the knowledge and skills of others and no one is left behind to complete the work alone.

What Do I Do?

This strategy for interaction and engagement can be used in any subject area. The teacher creates a set of tasks that must be completed by other students in the class. Each student receives a copy of the walking review sheet that is comprised of individual boxes containing a question and a place for obtaining a signature. Because a goal of this strategy is to promote conversation with a number of peers, a classmate can complete only one item per sheet. A final item is reserved for the owner of the sheet. This serves as an excellent means for classroom management because the teacher can gauge how many are finished by monitoring the number of students who have returned to their seats. A sample walking review from a writing class appears in Form 43.1 at the end of this chapter.

Now You Try It

Select tasks for review by your students and use the blank template in Form 43.2 at the end of this chapter. Be sure to model the process the first time so that students will understand the assignment. Discuss in advance what to do when you cannot locate someone who knows the answer or when a classmate provides an incorrect answer. By thoroughly modeling these scenarios you are more likely to prevent difficulties that may arise.

Walking Review Sample

1. Write a sentence that begins with *because*.	2. Write a word that ends with the letter *g*.
Name: _____	Name: _____
3. Write a sentence that lists three items.	4. Write a sentence that contains the word *information*.
Name: _____	Name: _____
5. Write a sentence that contains the words *but* and *for*.	6. Write a word that has two *r*'s in it.
Name: _____	Name: _____

Now here's one for you to do:

7. Write a sentence using the word written in box #2.

Walking Review Template

Name: _____ Date: _____

Directions: Find a classmate who can complete *one* of these writing tasks. Ask him or her to write the answer in the box and sign his or her name. You can do the same on your classmate's paper. When the boxes are completed you should have six names collected. Then answer question #7 yourself.

1.	2.
Name: _____	Name: _____
3.	4.
Name: _____	Name: _____
5.	6.
Name: _____	Name: _____

Now here's one for you to do:

7.

44

Jigsaws

GRADE LEVELS: K–12

Time Needed: Variable

What Is It?

The jigsaw method of small-group discussion has two distinct stages (Aronson, Blaney, Stephin, Sikes, & Snapp, 1978). In one part of a jigsaw, students work in expert groups, with the goal of understanding a section of text. They read and discuss the main ideas and the supporting details with one another, asking questions to clarify their understanding. Once the expert groups are satisfied that they are comfortable with the information and can report it accurately, each returns to his or her home group. The home group is comprised of a representative from each expert group. Together, each of the four members of the home group shares the information he or she learned in his or her expert group. Members of the home group take notes and ask questions, seeking to synthesize the information. For example, seventh-grade art teacher Mr. Bradshaw established four expert groups to participate in a jigsaw discussion of:

- **Line**—An identifiable path of a point moving in space.
- **Perspective**—The feeling of depth through the use of lines.
- **Value**—Shadows, darkness, contrasts, and light are all values.
- **Composition**—The arrangement of lines, colors, and form.

Students worked in groups of four to read and discuss information about these art terms and then returned to a home group of four to share and learn about each term. Mr. Bradshaw gave each student a note-taking guide, a piece of paper folded into four quadrants, to foster recall (Figure 44.1 is an example). They included their

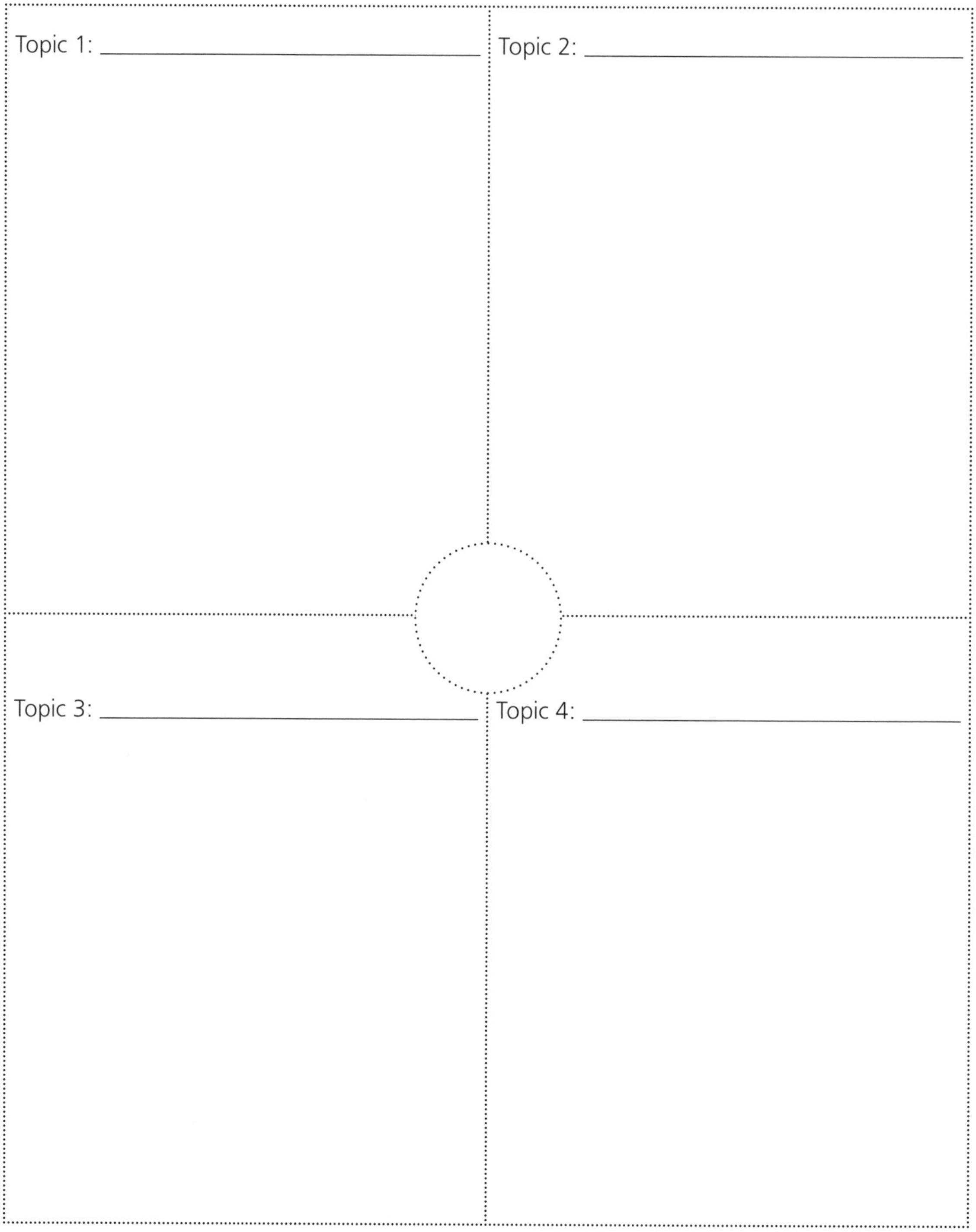

Topic 1: _____   Topic 2: _____

Topic 3: _____   Topic 4: _____

FIGURE 44.1. Discussion Note-Taking Guide. From *The English Teacher's Companion, Second Edition: Complete Guide to Classrooms, Curriculum, and the Profession* by Jim Burke. Copyright 2003 by Jim Burke. Published by Heinemann, Portsmouth, NH. All rights reserved.

own notes in the upper-left-hand quadrant and then took notes as their peers presented in the remaining quadrants.

What Do I Do?

A jigsaw requires some preparation. First, you must identify a piece of text worthy of this instructional routine. The selected text must have divisions that are about the same length and that do not require sequential reading. Informational texts that are divided into unique sections or different pieces of texts for each expert group work best. Second, you have to group students according to the number of topics to be covered. The expert groups and the home-base groups must be diverse enough to facilitate interaction and encourage conversation. And finally, time must be allocated for students to read and discuss the text. This may mean that additional time is consumed, but the trade-off is that students will really understand the text. Using a jigsaw process ensures that students receive multiple exposures to new vocabulary and ideas as they read, question and discuss, listen, retell, and write.

Now You Try It

As with many of the instructional routines in this book, a jigsaw should be modeled and demonstrated for students. Unlike some of the routines in this book, a jigsaw may require a few attempts before students master the process. Having said that, it's worth the wait as student interaction increases and they learn how to interact with one another.

Reference

Aronson, J., Blaney, N., Stephin, C., Sikes, J., & Snapp, M. (1978). *The jigsaw classroom.* Beverly Hills, CA: Sage.

45

Self-Corrected Spelling

GRADE LEVELS: K–8

Time Needed: 15 minutes

What Is It?

Effective spelling instruction is developmental and features hands-on, engaging activities that teach students systematically about orthographic and derivational patterns (Bear, Invernizzi, Templeton, & Johnston, 2004). Spelling activities should be linked to vocabulary development and word study so that students learn the meaning and use of the words as well as the correct spelling (Frey & Fisher, 2006). A challenge is to provide meaningful practice as students learn their spelling words. Self-corrected spelling is a way to provide practice that is hands-on and improves performance through attention to errors (Henderson, 1990).

What Do I Do?

Fearn and Farnan (2001) suggest using a game to practice spelling words for a few minutes every day to increase accuracy.

1 **Administer the spelling words as usual.** Ask students to write each word from their list as you state the word, use it in a sentence, and repeat the word.

2 **Write the words on the board and chant them.** Spell the words in unison.

3 **Have students self-correct their spelling words using an editing code.** This is the heart of the strategy. Instruct students to look at each word from left to right and draw a shape around each error. An error is considered to be a substitution, deletion, or insertion of a letter. Draw a □ (square) around the first error, a O (circle) around the second, and a △ (triangle) around the third. If there is a fourth error in the word, begin again with a square.

4 **Grade each word.** Have students assign a grade for themselves next to each word using the following grading scale:

- **A:** no errors
- **B:** 1–2 errors
- **C:** 3–4 errors

These grades are not recorded in your book; students are grading themselves. The value in this is that students are paying close attention to *each* error. With a traditional practice test, most students look only at words as being right or wrong but do not focus on the errors (Fearn & Farnan, 2001).

5 **Administer the words again.** Ask students to turn over the page and administer the words again. Give students time to self-correct again and ask for a show of hands to indicate improved performance from the first administration.

6 **Repeat every day until the spelling test.** Take a few minutes each day to repeat steps 1 through 4 to provide students with practice at self-corrected spelling. Performance will continue to rise with each session.

Now You Try It

Use a self-corrected practice test every day before the spelling test. You can decide whether students who achieve a 90% can skip the daily practice session. Use self-corrected practice tests as part of a developmental spelling program to improve spelling performance.

References

Bear, D. R., Invernizzi, M., Templeton, S., & Johnston, F. (2004). *Words their way: Word study for phonics, vocabulary, and spelling instruction.* Upper Saddle River, NJ: Pearson Merrill Prentice-Hall.

Fearn, L., & Farnan, N. (2001). *Interactions: Teaching writing and the language arts.* Boston: Houghton Mifflin.

Frey, N., & Fisher, D. (2006). *Language arts workshop: Purposeful reading and writing instruction.* Upper Saddle River, NJ: Merrill Prentice-Hall.

Henderson, E. H. (1990). *Teaching spelling* (2nd ed.). Boston: Houghton Mifflin.

46

Power Writing to Build Fluency

GRADE LEVELS: 2–8; ENGLISH CLASSES

Time Needed: 5 minutes per day

What Is It?

Power writing is a way to improve writing fluency through brief, timed writing events (Fearn & Farnan, 2001). The goal is to get students to put ideas down on paper rapidly. Power writing is typically a simple daily routine involving three 1-minute rounds of writing. Students keep a notebook or journal containing all of their writing, including the total number of words written for each topic. Students are reminded to "write as much as you can, as well as you can" (p. 196). A word or phrase is posted on the board, and students are asked to use it somewhere in their writing. The timer is set, and writing begins until it rings a minute later. When time is up, students reread what they have written, circling any errors they notice, then count and record the number of words in the margin. This routine is repeated two more times, until there are three 1-minute writing samples in their journals. Over time, as students graph their progress, they become more adept at putting down ideas on paper.

What Do I Do?

In my experience, students are very interested in this instructional routine as they find it fun, like a game. They set targets to improve their performance and work to increase their fluency (Fisher & Frey, 2007). Power writing starts with a topic, which can be a word or a phrase depending on the current course content. For example, to check their understanding of homophones, a teacher had students write using *they're* for one of the minutes, then *there* for the second minute, and finally *their* for the last round. Another teacher wanted to check her students' vocabulary knowledge and asked them to write about representative democracy in one of the rounds.

Once the topics have been identified, power writing is fairly easy to implement as students learn the routine. As their teacher, you'll want to monitor the total number of words written to ensure that students' fluency rates are improving. You'll also want to monitor the errors that students fail to notice in their writing. These errors are indicators of instructional needs, clearly demonstrating both an error and a lack of awareness about the error.

Now You Try It

To introduce this routine to your students, you might want to ask them to select a topic and write in front of them, modeling the procedures you'd like for them to use. Once they understand the procedures, you can select topics and engage students in thinking and writing about the coursework, while also improving their overall writing fluency.

References

Fearn, L., & Farnan, N. (2001). *Interactions: Teaching writing and the language arts*. Boston: Houghton Mifflin.

Fisher, D., & Frey, N. (2007). *Scaffolding writing instruction: A gradual release model*. New York: Scholastic.

PART SIX

Engaging Students through Reading

47

Choral Reading

GRADE LEVELS: K–8

Time Needed: 2–15 minutes

What Is It?

Choral reading is the practice of reading in unison. Groups of students perform a rehearsed passage together to build fluency and prosody. Reading in unison builds teamwork and positive attitudes toward reading, especially among those reluctant to read aloud on their own (Opitz & Rasinski, 1998). It is an alternative to round robin reading (individual students take turns reading a portion of a text), which has been found to reinforce ineffective reading behaviors (Allington, 1980; Opitz & Rasinski, 1998).

Keep in mind that asking students to read "cold" text is not helpful, and in fact interferes with comprehension. Choral-reading responses should always occur after the students have had an opportunity to read the text silently. This may occur after the teacher has modeled the reading, or after they have had a chance to read the passage to themselves. Choral reading is used for dramatic texts, such as Shakespearean plays, as well as times when poetic language forms take center stage.

What Do I Do?

♦ **Choose engaging texts to be read aloud.** Poems, rhymes, and narrative passages with dialogue are good choices for choral reading because students experience the rhythms used by the author. Textbooks are another good source of choral-reading passages. Take note of the sidebars that feature interesting anecdotal information.

◆ **Keep the passages short.** Choral reading should not go on for pages and pages. Passages can range from one or two sentences to as many as 100 to 150 words. Choose passages that allow you to focus attention on punctuation, word choice, vocabulary, or text features.

◆ **Read the passage silently first.** A criticism of round robin reading is that it interferes with comprehension because students struggle to coordinate decoding, pronunciation, and fluency all at the same time. Instruct students to read the passage to themselves, then discuss the meaning of the text.

◆ **Model and rehearse.** Passages should always be read first by the teacher, who is the fluent language model for the class. Place a copy of the text on the overhead projector and note the phrase boundaries and pauses. Rehearse several times to reinforce teaching points.

Now You Try It

Choral reading can be implemented in a variety of ways, depending on the features of the passage.

- ◆ **Call and response.** Split the class in half and assign alternating parts.
- ◆ **Radio reading.** Experiment with lines and words that are spoken loudly and softly, quickly and slowly, or with high and low voices. These changes in prosody should always be related to the meaning of the text (e.g., a bear's voice might sound low).
- ◆ **Dialogue reading.** Select a passage with dialogue and assign groups to chorally read the lines of each character. This provides students with an opportunity to hear the conversation as it occurs.

References

Allington, R. (1980). Teacher interruption behaviors during primary grade oral reading. *Journal of Educational Psychology, 72,* 371–372.

Opitz, M. F., & Rasinski, T. V. (1998). *Good-bye round robin: 25 effective oral reading strategies.* Portsmouth, NH: Heinemann.

48

Cloze Reading

GRADE LEVELS: K–12

Time Needed: 5–15 minutes

What Is It?

The cloze procedure has been described as a "fill-in-the-blank" process. It activates prior knowledge by challenging the reader to consider both the syntactic and semantic (grammatical and meaning, respectively) structures of the sentence (McKenna, 1990). Cloze reading is performed to engage students during teacher-led oral readings. Cloze reading can also be used to emphasize key ideas, such as when a character makes an especially insightful statement. In a textbook passage the cloze reading may be used to target key vocabulary.

What Do I Do?

1 **Choose a passage to be read aloud by the teacher.** This can be a portion of a book or textbook, written directions for an assignment, or an informational reading. Underline or highlight words you will be omitting from your reading.

2 **Distribute copies to students.** All students need a copy of the text.

3 **Introduce the cloze process.** Tell students you will pause occasionally while reading so that they can read the next word aloud.

4 **Instruct students to read in their heads while you read aloud.** Ask students to point to the first word of the passage you will be reading to ensure they begin in the right place. Remind them to follow along so they can accurately read the next word when you pause.

5 **Omit key words and phrases for emphasis.** Read at a natural rate and pace, pausing at highlighted words. Students should chorally read the following word. For example:

TEACHER: All insects use their mouths for (*pauses*) . . .

CLASS: Feeding.

TEACHER: Some insects are (*pauses*) . . .

CLASS: Hunters

TEACHER: And catch small animals for (*pauses*) . . .

CLASS: Food. (Glover, 1998, p. 12)

Now You Try It

Cloze reading can also be implemented using a passage with omitted words (Barr, Blachowicz, Katz, & Kaufman, 2002). This looks much like a fill-in-the-blank assignment but is read together as a class. To create a cloze passage, select a piece of text and type it into a word-processing program. Leave the first sentence intact and then substitute every fifth word with a blank. Place the prepared text on the overhead and read it aloud. Pause when you come to a blank and invite students to offer suggestions that are syntactically and semantically correct. Discuss the clues students use to arrive at the words, including background knowledge, information in other sentences, and inferences.

References

Barr, R., Blachowicz, C. L. Z., Katz, C., & Kaufman, B. (2002). *Reading diagnosis for teachers: An instructional approach* (4th ed.). New York: Allyn & Bacon.

Glover, D. (1998). *Looking at insects.* Barrington, IL: Rigby.

McKenna, M. (1990). Concurrent validity of cloze as a measure of intersentential comprehension. *Journal of Educational Psychology, 82,* 372–377.

49

Read-Around

GRADE LEVELS: K–6

Time Needed: 15–20 minutes

What Is It?

In a read-around, students select a favorite portion of a text to read aloud to other students in their group (Tompkins, 2004). This technique is ideally suited for literature circles and guided-reading groups because they share a common text. These student selections are sometimes called golden lines and are intended to prompt discussion about why the quote was chosen.

What Do I Do?

◆ **Provide time to reread the passage silently.** The read-around is done with familiar text, so begin the lesson with a silent rereading of the text.

◆ **Model the choice of a meaningful quote.** Choose a quote or paragraph that contains important information and explain your rationale for your selection.

◆ **Give students a sticky note to mark their selection.** After locating their choice, students mark it with a sticky note.

◆ **Rehearse the quote or passage that has been selected.** Students read the quote using a soft voice several times.

◆ **Direct students to share their golden lines.** Ask students to tell the group the page and paragraph location for the golden lines selected. Students take turns reading their choice aloud while other members follow along. They conclude by sharing the rationale for the choice.

Engaging Students through Reading

Now You Try It

Read-arounds are useful with informational text as well as narrative. Have students rewrite their quotation to serve as a central feature for a poster, shadow box, collage, or mobile. Deep exploration of the meaning of key sentences expands comprehension of a subject.

Reference

Tompkins, G. (2004). *Fifty literacy strategies: Step by step* (2nd ed.). Upper Saddle River, NJ: Merrill.

50

Rapid Retrieval of Information

GRADE LEVELS: 4–12

Time Needed: 2–10 minutes

What Is It?

Students need to be able to skim and scan reading passages quickly to locate information efficiently. Adults use this strategy daily to read a newspaper, web pages, directories, maps, and other reference materials. The practice of moving the eyes quickly across pages is foreign to many students, who view reading as something that is done word by word. Rapid retrieval of information (RRI) is an activity to provide students with opportunities to practice locating sentences quickly (Green, 1997/1998). This is an excellent strategy for use with tests featuring informational and narrative reading passages.

What Do I Do?

◆ **Select a text passage for practicing RRI.** Begin with shorter passages (100 to 200 words) that are written at a developmentally appropriate level for students. The length can be increased as students become more proficient at skimming and scanning.

◆ **Read the passage silently.** Students read the entire passage silently to allow time for them to understand the overall meaning.

◆ **Introduce RRI.** Tell students they will be using their eyes to move quickly over the passage they have just read to locate information. The goal is to find the correct sentence as quickly as possible. When they find the information requested, they are to put their finger or pencil on the words and raise their hand.

◆ **Ask questions to locate a specific phrase or sentence in the passage.** Pose questions that focus on information at the literal or inferential level.

> ◆ Find the sentence that gives a definition of *photosynthesis*.
>
> ◆ Locate the phrase the *Wicked Witch* used to address the mirror.
>
> ◆ One stanza of the poem discusses winter. What is the poet's opinion of winter? Point to the words that support your answer.

◆ **Elicit a response.** Instruct students to turn to their response partner to answer the question. Check to see whether your partner is pointing to the correct answer.

Now You Try It

Model skimming and scanning by placing text on the document presenter. Teach students that an efficient way to skim and scan is by first determining what word or phrase you are seeking. Use a pen to highlight the key words and phrases. Variations of RRI can include using a timer, working in reading partners, or letting students lead instruction with classmates.

Reference

Green, M. (1997/1998). Rapid retrieval of information: Reading aloud with a purpose. *Journal of Adolescent and Adult Literacy, 41,* 306–307.

Index